DIGITAL TECHNOLOGIES AND TEACHING STRATEGIES

DIGITAL TECHNOLOGIES AND TEACHING STRATEGIES

Editor
V.C. Pandey

ISHA BOOKS
DELHI—110 033

Digital Technologies and Teaching Strategies
(Education, Information Technology)

ISBN: 81-8205-049-9

Published in 2006 in India by
Isha Books, D-43, Prithviraj Road
Adarsh Nagar, Delhi-110 033

Lasertypesetting by: Varsha Graphics, Delhi
Printed at: **Sudha Offset Press, Delhi.**

Contents

Preface

Like all other professions, teachers need constant and continuous renewal to be effective, motivated, and up to date in their knowledge and skills. While this is not a mandatory requirement in many national jurisdictions, those that do have such requirements use and see information and communication technologies (ICTs) as important vehicles to provide continuing professional development to teachers.

With ICTs, sharing knowledge resources is enhanced many times over. Putting information on the World wide Web makes it available immediately to anyone in the world with a suitable connection. Teachers can share lesson plans with their colleagues in their own jurisdictions and with those far removed from their jurisdictions. Students from all over the world can undertake joint projects, exchange findings, analyse data collectively, and draw reasoned conclusions.

This book is an attempt to frame the applications of digital technologies in teaching. It draws on worldwide knowledge and experience to delineate the potentials of ICTs for teaching, the parameters for turning this potential into effectiveness, and the prospects of applying these capacities in different environments.

Editor

1

Online Teaching Strategies

The on-line technology allows for networking across the large distances and provides the opportunity for people working in diverse school situations to learn from each other through the discussion of cases drawn from the everyday experience of principals working across the diversity of schools. Case-based instruction has a long history in education for leadership and administration. It originated as an instructional technique at Harvard University Law School in 1870 and later became widely accepted in a variety of professional disciplines. A case as an account or description of a situation or sequence of events confronting an individual, a group of individuals, or an organization. Rather than deliver concepts and theories, cases also called clinical correlation, leadership stories, real-life narratives, critical incidents, and vignettes present situations for analysis about which decisions must be made.

There are similarities of structure between case histories, clinical cases, problem-based learning and other experientially based methods in that they are all oriented to the particularities of practice while drawing on the generalities of theory. The purpose of cases and case-based instruction in any professional field relates directly to the nature of the body of knowledge that exists in that particular field. For example, in teacher education cases are used to develop reflective practitioners and to promote teacher reflection and enhanced understanding. In the field of educational administration where decision-making skills are crucial, cases can offer opportunities to practice analysis, problem solving, action planning, and evaluation. In the educational studies in general and in the area of school administration in particular the interest in the case methodology is manifested through a wide incorporation of and experimentation with case-based instruction in pre-service and in-service training of teachers and administrators. At the university level, special centers have been established for research and promotion of the case methodology in the field of education. Likewise, educational journals devote a great deal of attention to this matter and provide a forum for discussion of the value of case methodology for preparation of educational cadre. For example, The Journal of Cases in Educational Leadership (JCEL) published by University of Utah is devoted solely to the publication of cases that can be effectively used in preparation of educational leaders.

Principal preparation programs have used case studies to remedy problems that arise in the gap between theory and practice. A major criticism of principal preparation programs has been: "Regardless of the year appointed, have been trained and certified as administrators through programs largely irrelevant to and grossly inadequate for the work responsibilities found in the school principalship". The case methodology combines both artifactual and social elements. The artifactual component is the case itself, a description of an actual situation.

The emergence of computer-based technologies opened up new possibilities for case conferencing. The collision of technology and case methodology was inevitable. The combination of technology and case-based instruction gave birth to new applications of case methodology in teacher and principal preparation programs, for example video-cases, computer-based simulations, virtual case competitions on the World Wide Web, cases presented as CD-ROM and laser disks, and electronic meeting systems. The technological formats of case analysis can be written, spoken, or based in hypermedia utilizing the Internet or World Wide Web. Unlike the traditional classroom discussion of cases, electronic meeting systems (EMS) allow for constant ongoing dialogue between participants. Moreover, electronic brainstorming produces significantly more fresh ideas than traditional classroom analysis of cases. EMS also allows more people to interact without interruption and to input ideas simultaneously.

Opportunity for the participation of all group members is also enhanced in computer-mediated case discussions. On-line case discussion in the York University PQP resonates with the need to decrease the gap between classroom instruction and practice and to enhance students' ability to make good decisions that are at the core of school leadership. The PQP on-line cases are experiential narratives that focus on a broad set of concerns specific to the work of the principal. The cases, referred to by participants as scenarios, problems or situations, are posted weekly by the On-Line Mentors.

Each week, candidates read the posted cases and respond to the issues, events and dilemmas of the case taking the perspective of a principal. This requires them to shift their reading of the cases from their experiential teaching horizon toward a one that encompasses the relationships within the school, the school community and the educational system with it's diverse participants. The role of case discussion facilitator is important in case methodology generally and the York PQP specifically.

The facilitator guides the discussion by probing, directly challenging, or simply observing the discussion process. Feedback plays an important role in the learning process: as people receive information about the results of their actions, they are able to correct themselves progressively until they achieve the intended results. The PQP On-Line Mentors, all of whom were classroom teachers prior to becoming a principal, bring their knowledge of teaching and learning to the CMC environment. They provide feedback in the form of comments addressed to candidates' responses, suggestions for different presentation strategies, ideas for deepening the responses, or concluding thoughts. The On-Line Mentors also direct discussions and monitor candidates' participation in order to facilitate discussions that are reflective and thoughtful. In order to make case discussions challenging, educative and interesting, On-Line Mentors may make suggestions and ask questions related to the posted case.

The on-line narratives are written rather than oral interactions, often presented in a laconic and point specific form rather than lengthy and comprehensive manner. The audiences for whom the narratives are constructed are other educators attending or teaching the course. Although one face-to-face meeting of the on-line groups is scheduled during the course, candidates may never meet their on-line mentor or other members of their on-line group. Group cohesion is developed through a combination of required participation, the skill of the on-line mentor, and the ongoing involvement of the participants.

Case methodology has changed in recent years from the method of instruction based on face-to-face discussion of oral cases/narratives confined to the classroom space to computer-mediated asynchronous discussion of on-line cases in virtual classrooms/cyber-classrooms. Narratives in cyberspace, rather than being a part of an oral discourse, entail new communicative styles and ways of engagement with texts/cases on the part of the learners. In theorizing of learning, claims have been made that we learn from the other's response to what we convey. Thus, learning the art of school leadership through on-line narratives necessitates the learners to put their responses out there and to find out what comes back.

A unique feature of the York PQP cases posted on-line is that often they present an account of events that happened in the same week (or sometimes even the same day) as the case is posted for discussion. While varying in content and length, the cases are authentic narratives from the work experience of GTA principals. As such, they have some pedagogical similarity to more traditional principal training methods such as "inbox" and "shadowing" exercises. Some of the cases posted by On-Line Mentors open up with the words like: "Just a quick situation we had at our school this week that caused us some thought" or "Here is the situation based on a real case that happened recently." The fact that cases posted for discussion are "fresh" cases enables On-Line Mentors to enrich the dialogue by adding new details and nuances to the case and informing participants about the trajectory of events.

The use of narratives brings into view the implicit and explicit ethical and moral issues that permeate the stories of schooling. Narratives bring the complexity of the coordinated stories about school leadership and administration to the medium of on-line group learning. Equally important, they allow beginners "to consider and inspect the informal or tacit systems which exist side-by-side with the formal manifest systems operating in schools and organizations'. One of the program challenges that confront PQP candidates and their program teachers are to develop the skill to see the case narratives through the eyes of an administrator rather than a teacher. In the on-line mentor responses, we see a complex teaching and learning about the social and professional mores of the principalship.

As the course progresses, candidates felt freer to speak from their professional experiences in the teaching profession and from their life experiences as people interested in education. Bringing their life experiences to bear on an administrative framework, students came up with diverse (often even polar) responses and felt free to disagree with one another. The consensual uniformity of candidates' standpoints was less present in the analysis of the cases that dealt with ethical concerns or involved moral judgements. The analysis of the PQP on-line narratives, student responses to less complex and more transparent cases often resulted in producing collective virtual texts where each ensuing individual script, more or less, echoed the line of thinking developed in responses posted earlier. In contrast, the responses to case narratives that drew on local experience with ethical issues embedded in the stories did not turn into unitary, virtual texts—one-best solution—produced by collective efforts of on-line participants.

Large-Scale Assessment and Internet

Depending upon the type of test, the issues precipitating change include an outmoded cognitive-scientific basis for test design; a mismatch with curriculum; the differential performance of population groups; a lack of information to help individuals improve; and inefficiency. These issues provide a strong motivation to reconceptualize both the substance and the business of large-scale assessment. At the same time, advances in technology, measurement, and cognitive science are providing the means to make that reconceptualization a reality. In the same way that it is already helping to revolutionize commerce, education, and even social interaction, the Internet will help revolutionize the business and substance of large-scale assessment.

Whether for educational admissions, school and student accountability, or public policy, large-scale assessment in the United States is undergoing enormous pressure to change. This pressure is most evident with respect to high-stakes tests, like those used for grade promotion or college entrance. For achievement surveys like NAEP, which offer no information to individuals, schools, or districts, motivation to participate is undoubtedly diminished. Testing programs are expensive to operate. That expense gets passed on to taxpayers for a state or federal test like NAEP, or directly to examinees in the case of admissions measures. Further, to be maximally useful, test results are needed quickly.

Rapid information delivery is certainly a requirement in the education policy arena, where the results of national surveys may sometimes take years to produce. It is also increasingly true in the admissions context, where more rapid feedback is needed not only for early decisions, financial aid, and the rolling acceptances that are beginning to characterize some distance learning programs, but also for guidance and placement. Radical improvements in assessment will derive from advances in three areas: technology, measurement, and cognitive science. Of the three, new technology will be the most influential in the short term.

New technology will have the greatest influence because it—not measurement and not cognitive science—is pervading our society. Billions of dollars are being invested annually to create and make commonplace powerful, general technologies for commerce, communications, entertainment, and education. Due to their generality, these technologies can also be used to improve assessment. These technological advancements revolve primarily around the Internet. The Internet is (or will be) interactive, broadband, switched, networked, and standards-based. Interactive means that we can present a task to a student and quickly respond to that student's actions. Switched means that we can engage in different interactions with different students simultaneously.

In combination, these two characteristics (interactive and switched) make for individualized assessments. Broadband means that those interactions can contain lots of information. For assessment tasks, that information could include audio, video, and animation. Networked indicates that everything is linked. This linkage means that testing agencies, schools, parents, government officials, item writers, test reviewers, human scorers, and students are tied together electronically. That electronic connection can allow for enormous efficiencies. The standards-based means that the network runs according to a set of conventional rules that all participants follow. That fact permits both the easy interchange of data and access from a wide variety of computing platforms, as long as the software running on those platforms (e.g., Internet browsers), adheres to those rules too.

Internet affords the potential to deliver efficiently on a mass scale individualized, highly engaging content to almost any desktop; get data back immediately; process it; and make information available anywhere in the world, anytime day or night. Paper delivery cannot compete with this potential. The Internet is, of course, not being built to service the needs of large-scale assessment. It is, instead, being built for e-commerce: to sell products and services over the web to consumers and to businesses directly. Coincidentally, the capabilities needed for e-commerce are essentially those needed for e-assessment:

— interactive (so that products can be offered and orders transacted),

— switched (so different business transactions can be conducted with different customers simultaneously),

— broadband (so that those offers can be as engaging and enticing as possible),

— networked (so that product offers, orders, shipping, inventory, and accounting can be integrated), and

— standards-based (so that everyone can get to it, regardless of computing platform).

By any measure, the Internet and use of it, has grown dramatically, to say the least. As a communications medium, the Internet last year surpassed the telephone, with 3 billion email messages sent each day. The number of unique URLs (web-page directory and subdirectory addresses) has grown from just under a billion in 1998 to a projected 3 billion in 2000. In the United States, the percentage of homes with Internet access has increased from 26% in December 1998 to 42% in August 2000. Worldwide, the number of users has grown from somewhere between 117 to 142 million in 1998 to about 400 million in 2000.

Finally, the number of host computers has gone from about 30 million to 75 million from January 1998 to January 2000. This phenomenal growth may slow as investment subsides from the speculative rates of the past few years. However, the vast size of the Internet and its user base constitute a critical mass that should continue to attract substantial capital. For commerce, the promise of the Internet is all about being faster, cheaper, and better. Two "laws" of the digital era illustrate this promise. Moore's Law predicts the doubling of computational capability (specifically, at the level of the microchip) every 18 months. The true value of a network is, thus, less about information and more about community. One can see this effect clearly in eBay, the online auction broker. Each new user potentially benefits every other existing user because every eBay member can be both buyer and seller. Metcalfe's law is playing out well beyond eBay. Online business-to-business auction brokers are appearing in a variety of industries, including natural gas, electricity, steel, and bandwidth. Another illustration of this cheaper-faster-better result is the effect of the Internet on the traditional relationship between richness and reach, where richness is the depth of the interaction that a business can have with a customer and reach is the number of customers that a business can contact through a given channel.

Traditionally, one limited the other. That is, a business could attain maximal reach but only limited richness. For example, through direct mail, broadcast, or newspaper ads a company could communicate with many people but have a meaningful interaction with none of them. Similarly, a business could attain maximal richness but limited reach. Via personal contact (e.g., door-to-door sales), very deep interactions can occur, but with only a relatively small number of people. What has the Internet done? It has transformed the relationship between richness and reach by allowing businesses to touch many people in a personalized but inexpensive way. It makes for mass customization.

There are two major dimensions to reinventing assessment. One is the business of assessment. This dimension centers on the core processes that define an enterprise. In many cases, those core processes can become many times more efficient because moving bits is faster and easier than moving atoms; that is, electronically processing information is far more cost effective than physically manipulating things.

For large-scale testing programs, some examples of the potential for electronic processing are in:

— developing tests, making the items easier to review, revise, and automatically morph into still more items because the items themselves are digitally represented;

— delivering tests, eliminating the costs of printing, warehousing, and shipping tons of paper;
— presenting dynamic stimuli like audio, video, and animation, making the need for specialized testing equipment (e.g., audio cassette recorders, VCRs) obsolete;
— transmitting some types of complex constructed responses to human graders, removing the need to transport, house, and feed the graders;
— scoring other complex constructed responses automatically, reducing the need for human reading et al.,; and
— distributing test results, cutting the costs of printing and mailing reports.

Encyclopaedia Britannica was established in Scotland in 1768. It is the oldest and most famous encyclopedia in the English-speaking world. By 1990, its sales had reached $650 million per annum. But then suddenly, Britannica's fortunes drastically changed. In 1996, the company was sold for less than half its net worth (i.e., the value of its assets, including its encyclopedia inventory, minus its liabilities). That same year, it eliminated its entire door-to-door North American sales force. What happened was that the reference book business was reinvented because of the emergence of new technology. At its peak, Britannica was a 32-volume set of books costing well over $1,000.

In 1993, Microsoft introduced Encarta on CD-ROM for under $100 and even though Britannica was much more comprehensive, the difference for most people wasn't worth an extra $900+. Initially, Britannica did not respond as it didn't take the threat from Encarta seriously. But when it did respond, it did so ineffectively because Britannica wouldn't fit on a single CD-ROM and because the company's large sales force wasn't suited to selling software.

But, ultimately, Britannica wasn't ready to cannibalize its existing paper business to enter this new electronic one. Why is this story important? It's important because similar (though less extreme) scenarios are playing themselves out now in individual investing, book selling, travel planning, music distribution, long distance telephony, and even business-to-business transactions. (As to the last, Cisco Systems makes 90% of its revenue from business-to-business transactions done over the Internet.

These reinvention scenarios are forcing organizations—including some in educational assessment—to come quickly to grips with where new technology will and will not help core business processes. As should be obvious, technology-driven changes in business processes can occur quickly and their consequences can be significant for the organizations that service a particular market. In fact, if radical and pervasive enough, process changes can force shifts in the substance of the business itself.

So, although reinventing the business of assessment by incorporating technology into specific assessment processes is about trying to achieve the efficiencies needed to remain competitive today, reinventing the substance of assessment—most fundamentally, the reason we do it—is not about today. It's about tomorrow.

The populations seeking education are changing and so are their purposes for learning. At the college level, just 16% of students fit the traditional profile: 18-22 years old, full-time, on-campus resident. This is not because fewer 18-22 year olds are going to college. It is because more adults are. The adult cohort is, in fact, the fastest growing segment in postsecondary education.

Working adults over age 24 constitute some 44% of college students. Over the past 25 years, employer demand in the U.S. has shifted toward higher educational qualifications, as indicated by an increasing premium paid for those with a college degree. But in addition to this rise in entry qualifications, the knowledge required to maintain a job in many occupations is changing so fast that 50% of all employees' skills are estimated to become outdated within 3-5 years.

Witness any job that requires interaction with information technology (IT), which is a growing proportion of jobs. In fact, by 2006 almost half of all workers will be employed by industries that are either major producers or intensive users of IT products and services. So, more people want postsecondary education because they need to have it if they want to become—and stay—employed. And, more of these individuals are nontraditional students who may work, travel in their jobs, or have families. This population's unmet educational need is increasingly becoming the target of distance learning.

According to the National Center for Education Statistics, between fall 1995 and 1997-98, the percentage of higher education institutions offering distance learning courses increased by one-third, and the number of course offerings and enrollments approximately doubled. But although many institutions have delivered distance learning via mail, radio, or television for years, this growth is not in those media. Rather, it is distance learning via the Internet that is booming.

Among all higher-education institutions offering any distance learning, the percentage of institutions using asynchronous Internet-based technologies nearly tripled, from 22% in 1995 to 60% in 1997-1998. More recent data from Market Data Retrieval (MDR) confirm the trend. MDR relates that, as of the 1999-2000 academic year, 34% of two- and four-year colleges offered accredited degree programs via computer, up from 15% the year before. As of 2000, U.S. institutions reportedly offered more than 6,000 accredited courses on the Web and, by 2002, over 2 million students will be enrolled, a tripling of the 1998 enrollment. At the same time, Internet-based distance learning is finding its way into high school.

The need is generated by home-schooled students (of which there are over 1 million in the US), districts without a full complement of qualified teachers, and the children of migrant workers. So-called "virtual high schools" have emerged in Alabama, Arizona, California, Florida, Illinois, Indiana, Kentucky, Maryland, Massachusetts, Michigan, Missouri, Nebraska, New Mexico, and Utah. These programs can cross state lines, with offerings open to students regardless of residence. Of particular note is that both the University of Missouri at Columbia High School and the Indiana University High School have been granted accreditation by the North Central Association of Colleges and Schools. Accreditation means that students can apply course grades earned through these online institutions toward their high-school graduation.

The growth of Internet-based distance learning will have a significant impact upon traditional education. For one, it may threaten the existence of established institutions. Many in the private sector see education as a huge industry that produces mediocre results for a high cost. If the private sector can leverage new technologies, like distance learning, to deliver greater value, the institutions that dominate education today will not be the leaders tomorrow.

The rapid growth of for-profit education companies, and the seemingly endless creation of well-capitalized new ones, suggests that a serious challenge to the existing order is well underway. The gravity of the threat is evident in how non-profits have responded. A second reason that the growth of Internet-based distance learning will influence traditional education is that regardless of its impact on nonprofit institutions, the distance learning industry will produce sophisticated software that everyone can use, in school and out.

The considerable potential of online learning—local or distance—is reflected in a report to the President and Congress of the bipartisan Web-Based Education Commission. The question is no longer if the Internet can be used to transform learning in new and powerful ways. The Commission has found that it can. Nor is the question should we invest the time, the energy, and the money necessary to fulfill its promise in defining and shaping new learning opportunity. As online learning becomes more widespread, the substance and format of assessment will need to keep pace.

So, as students do more and more of their learning using technology tools, asking them to express that learning in a medium different from the one they typically work in will become increasingly untenable, especially where working with the medium is part of the skill being tested. These changes in learning methodology offer exciting possibilities for assessment innovation. On site or off, an obvious result of delivering courses via the Internet is the potential for embedding assessment, perhaps almost seamlessly, in instruction.

Since students respond to instructional exercises electronically, their responses can be recorded, leaving a continuous learning trace. Depending upon how the course and the assessment are designed, this information could conceivably support a sophisticated model of student proficiencies. That model might be useful both for dynamically deciding what instruction to present next and for making more global judgments about what the student knows and can do at any given point. In addition to assessment embedded in Internet-delivered courses, one can imagine Internet-delivered-assessment embedded in traditional classroom activity.

Such assessment might take the form of periodically delivered exercises that both teach and test. In this scenario, the exercises would be standardized and performance might serve, depending upon the level of aggregation, to indicate individual, classroom, school, district, state, or national achievement. Thus, these exercises could serve summative as well as formative purposes and be useful to individuals as well as institutions.

A continuing concern with such reinvention visions is whether schools (and students) are ready technologically and, in particular, what to do about technology differences across social groups. The National Center for Education Statistics (NCES) reports that as of September 1999, 95% of schools were connected to the Internet, up from 35% in 1994.

Schools in all categories, (i.e., by grade level, poverty concentration, and metropolitan status), were equally likely to have Internet access. Further, most schools had dedicated lines: only 14% were using dial-up modem, a slower and less reliable access method. Clearly many of these schools could have only a single connected machine and that machine could be the one sitting on the principal's desk.

According to NCES, as of September 1999, 63% of all instructional rooms had Internet access (up from 3% in 1994, a 20-fold increase in five years). The ratio of students to Internet-connected computers was 9:1, down from 12:1 only a year earlier. These are staggering numbers, for they imply that classrooms are connecting to the Internet at a very rapid rate. This success is in no small part due to federal efforts.

The government's e-rate program has been giving public schools and libraries discounts of up to 90% on phone service, Internet hook-ups, and wiring for several years. In total, the program has committed 3.65 billion dollars to over 50,000 institutions, helping connect more than one million public school classrooms. In addition, 70% of the program's last round of funding went to schools in the lowest income areas. However, even with these very significant efforts, there continue to be equity issues. As of September 1999, in high poverty schools, the ratio of students to Internet computers was 16 to 1. Certainly, with few exceptions, it would be impossible to deliver large-scale assessment via the Internet today. But the trend is clear: the infrastructure is quickly falling into place for Internet delivery of assessment to schools, perhaps first in survey programs like NAEP that require only a small participant sample from each school, but eventually for inclusive assessments delivered directly to the desktop.

As evidence, witness the requests-for-proposals recently released by the state education departments of Oregon, Virginia, and Georgia for building Internet-delivered, state-assessment systems. Assuming that every classroom is wired, will all students then have the technology skills needed to take tests on-line? Clearly, more students are becoming computer-familiar every day and developing such skills is a national educational technology goal.

But, as Negroponte suggests, computer familiarity is really the wrong issue. The secret to good interface design is to make it go away. Thus, advances in technology will eventually eliminate the need to be computer familiar. After nomadic computing, which we are now entering with the proliferation of wireless Internet devices and personal digital assistants, comes ubiquitous computing—the embedding of new technology into everyday items.

Inventions like "radio" paper may allow students to interact with computers in the same way that they interact with paper today. Smart desks are another likelihood, in which case a test may be electronically delivered, quite literally, to every desktop. Then, we may see a future in which every classroom is wired and every student can easily take tests on line.

To be sure, the Internet is an American phenomenon. It derives from research sponsored by the Defense Department in the 1960's. As a result of this history, the overwhelming majority of users were, until very recently, from US shores. At this writing, over 60% of Net users reside outside of the United States and the foreign growth rate now exceeds the domestic one. The largest numbers of foreign Internet users are, of course, in developed nations. These nations have the telecommunications infrastructure and citizens with enough disposable income to afford the trappings of Internet use.

The challenges for these nations are undoubtedly great. Over time, however, we should see significant progress in building the infrastructure and the user base here too. This progress will occur for at least two reasons. First, the cost of technology has been dropping precipitously and, by Moore's law, will continue to decline. Further, because the future of computing is undoubtedly in wireless devices, a telecommunications infrastructure will be much cheaper to acquire than the land-lines of old.

Metcalfe's law suggests, markets will become all the more valuable as they are interconnected. (Witness the global economy and the economic benefits resulting to nations from integration with it.) That developing nations join the e-commerce network means greater opportunity for all. It means more vendor choice for the people of developing nations; more opportunity for developed nations to serve these markets; and a new opportunity for third-world businesses themselves to compete globally.

The Internet will make it easier for developing nations to get access to assessment services from elsewhere and for those nations to distribute their own assessment services regionally or around the world. This ease of access and distribution should make it possible to form international consortia. Such consortia will be able to assemble technical resources that a single nation might not be able to acquire. In addition, those consortia may be able to purchase services from others more efficiently than nations could obtain individually.

Finally, an electronic network should make it easier to participate in international studies, bringing the benefits of benchmarking to nations throughout the world. One of the largest instantiations of technology-based assessment to date is computer-based testing (CBT) in postsecondary admissions. As programs like the Graduate Record Examinations, the Graduate Management Admission Test, and the Test of English as a Foreign Language have found, CBT can be enormously costly. Being among the first large-scale programs to move to computer, they bore the brunt of creating the infrastructure for what was essentially a new business.

The building of that infrastructure was initiated in the early 1990's before test developers knew how to create tests for computer, before computers were widely available for individuals to take tests on, and before the Internet was ready to bring those tests to students. In essence, these programs needed to build both a factory to stamp out a new product and a new distribution mechanism. A first generation infrastructure now exists, but it is not yet optimized to produce and deliver tests as efficiently as possible. If we have learned anything from the history of innovation, it is that new technologies are often initially far too expensive for mass use. That was true of the automobile, telephone service, commercial aviation, and the personal computer, among many other innovations.

For example, in 1930 the cost of a three-minute telephone call from New York to London was $250. By 1995, the cost had dropped to under $1. As a second instance, when the IBM Personal Computer was introduced in 1981, it cost around $5,000. At the time, the median family income in the United States was on the order of $25,000, so that a computer cost about 20% of the average family's earnings—not very affordable. At this writing, the cost of a computer with many times greater capability is a little more than $500 and the median income is closer to $55,000.

A computer now costs about 1% of average income. When a promising new technology appears, individuals and institutions invest, allowing the technology to evolve and a supporting infrastructure to develop. Over the course of that development, failures inevitably occur. Eventually, the technology either dies or becomes commercially viable—that is, efficient enough. At this point, it's an impressive list including non-profit testing agencies, for profit-testing companies, school districts, state education departments, government agencies, and companies with no history in testing at all.

Sustaining technologies enhance the performance of established products in ways that mainstream customers have traditionally valued. Historically, most technological advances in any given industry have been sustaining ones (e.g., in the personal computer industry, faster chips and bigger, higher-resolution monitors). Occasionally, disruptive technologies emerge. Companies introduce these technologies hoping their features will provide competitive edge. However, these features characteristically overshoot the market, giving customers more than they need or are willing to pay for. Thus, disruptive technologies result in worse product performance, at least in the near-term, on key dimensions in a company's established markets.

Interestingly, a few fringe customers typically find a disruptive technology's new features attractive. In these niche markets, such technology may thrive. If and when it advances to the level and nature of performance demanded in the mainstream market, the new technology can invade it, rapidly knocking out the traditional technology and its dependent practitioners. CBT has many of the characteristics of a disruptive technology. Established testing organizations are applying it in their mainstream markets, most notably postsecondary admissions. This innovation was introduced, in good part, to provide competitive edge through features like the ability to take a test at one's convenience and to get score reports immediately. As it turned out, these features overshot the market.

At least initially, registrations for continuously-offered computer-based admissions tests mirrored those for fixed-date administrations, suggesting that scheduling convenience was not a highly valued feature in the market of the time. Moreover, examinees were dissatisfied with losing some of the features of paper exams, including the ability to proceed through the test nonlinearly, the option to review the scoring of items actually taken, and the low cost. Although it encountered difficulty in the mainstream admissions testing market, CBT found more rapid acceptance in the niches.

One example is information technology (IT) certification, which individuals pursue to document their competence in some computer-related proficiency. In 1999, over three million examinations in 25 languages were administered in this market. Most of these tests were delivered on computer and most were offered on a continuous basis. Let's start by asking what features a testing product must have to succeed in this niche. First, it must be continuously offered because these test candidates build technology skill on their own schedules—at home or on the job, very often through books or online learning. These individuals want to test when they are ready, not when the testing companies are. Second, such a test must generally be offered on computer since technology use is the essence of the certification.

Security is not as critical as in admissions testing, so large item pools are not needed, reducing production cost. Lower security is tolerable because if an individual appears on the job with a dishonestly obtained credential but without the required skill, he or she will not last. Finally, test volume is self-replicating: there are many repeat test takers because information technology changes rapidly, so skills must be updated constantly. From an innovation perspective, then, IT certification may be one context in which the CBT of today can flourish and develop to better meet the needs of other assessment markets.

Industry leaders often fail precisely because they attempt to introduce disruptive technologies into major markets before it's time. The Industry leaders do not pursue those opportunities to refine the technology. Instead, they give up, having run out of resources or credibility. Making a disruptive technology work requires iteration and iteration means failure. Because they risk neither large resources nor reputations in the mainstream market, it is the fringe players who can fail early, often, and inexpensively enough to eventually challenge and overtake the industry leaders.

Issues of Education Technology

Ethical issues are surprisingly often lurking in technical

decisions. For example, reporting outcomes from a continuous measure in terms of the percent of students who surpassed a certain level, produces unethical behavior: a concentration of teaching on borderline students.

Distortion of behavior and data corruption are ever-present concerns in indicator systems. The systems we describe would have probably failed to thrive had they not addressed schools' on-going concerns about education. Moreover, data interpretation can only be completed in the schools, by those who know all the factors involved.

Over the last 15 years, indicator systems that have developed, and attracted support and subscriptions from about a third of the schools in England and also developed a linked Curriculum, Evaluation and Management Centre at the University of Canterbury in Christchurch, New Zealand, and have the pleasure of welcoming participation from scattered schools in thirty countries. The development of the indicator systems in the CEM Centre is unusual if not unique in that schools themselves have chosen to participate.

The systems are therefore professional, ground-up, developments, that stand in contrast to "top-down" indicator systems created, and sometimes imposed, by state and local authorities. The interests of both kinds of systems should ultimately, however, be coincident: to improve education. An indicator can be defined as an item of information collected at regular intervals to track the performance of a system. The indicator systems that have formed the basis of the learning are all designed to feed back valuable information of interest to teachers and administrators in schools and colleges.

The indicator or information systems as significantly empowering schools as they participate with a university in 'distributed research'. The issue of public accountability must also addressed by indicator systems. The design of each system has been driven by the need to measure outcomes that matter along with relevant covariates so that fair comparisons can be made. Process variables are measured in some of the systems, but only to generate hypotheses, not to make judgements. Technical issues include those procedural problems that must be solved if an indicator system is to be of high quality and run in a timely, efficient and effective fashion. Indicators need to be based on adequate samples, have appropriate levels of reliability, good validity, and above all, positive reactivity. These are technical terms straight out of research methods courses, but they go to the heart of indicator systems, and any practical use of data. The data must be of research quality, otherwise it will confuse rather than guide.

In 1983, technical sophistication was no more than batch-processing using a mainframe. The mainframe could deliver capital letters and stars and eventually an adequate type-face could be constructed via embedded commands in a special program that could produce quite nicely spaced upper and lower case printing. Access to a data entry service was essential and it was quickly obvious, as the volume of data increased, that adequate data verification techniques had to be built-in. At first, this was by double-entry, which was not satisfactory; followed by data checking on entry, which required some programming to prevent out-of-range data being entered and to ensure the data went into the right columns on the 80-column cards. From these humble and clumsy beginnings, today to a situation where extensive programming is used, optical mark recognition assists some data entry, computer based tests that can record responses directly and be delivered across intranets and internets are becoming essential features of indicator systems.

Not only is data translated into meaningful sentences contingent upon the data-values, but also into graphs that, for example, change colour when differences are statistically significant. Without this level of technical expertise, data will not be attractive and easy to access by busy teachers, the turn-around of data will be slow and errors will creep in. Schools want data quickly, within weeks of examination results becoming available. And they want the data 100 per cent accurate. In consequence, not only must there be teams of expert programmers, but also very high capacity computing equipment. Facilities for printing CDs are helpful, as special, user-friendly software is developed to assist schools in their own explorations of their data. CDs can also be used to deliver computerised tests.

The data files returned to schools also need to interface easily with schools' management information software such as timetabling and staff deployment. If the technical infrastructure is effective, data turn-around quick, data presentation attractive and readily interpreted, then the indicator systems will probably grow and this growth itself demands further technical capabilities, such as running a high-capacity server and creating a central database that can be accessed by researchers and secretaries alike. This central database needs to be relational in order to store efficiently the hundreds of thousands of students with hundreds of variables attached to each student in thousands of schools over many years. It must have an extremely friendly front end, so that secretaries can readily track the mail-out of questionnaires and the return of data, plus a massive invoicing system if individual schools can join the project and pay on their own account.

Finally the infrastructure needs communication on a regular basis with all schools. Newsletters, a website and conferences are important, particularly as teachers become conference presenters and have a credibility with fellow teachers that researchers lose after some years away from the classroom. If the infrastructure for indicator systems can be created, then a cost-effective system is feasible. It consider the design of such a system, including choosing what to measure, collecting the data, analysing, reporting and interpreting the data. A few indicators cannot reflect the complexity of institutions and will undermine the system as gaming takes hold. Given a few indicators, the effort is focused on these concerns alone.

Furthermore it is difficult to know which indicators will become important in the future, so that what is now considered to be a key indicator may become of less concern in the future. Multiple indicators for complex organisations are a fairer representation of the multiple realities within each than is any attempt to assign a single label, whether this label be numerical (e.g. average value added) or verbal (e.g. 'coasting', 'failing'). Bloom's Taxonomy of Educational Objectives identified affective, cognitive and psychomotor outcomes that can be taken to include behavioural outcomes. The distinction between aptitudes and achievements is an important distinction in the cognitive area. Clearly money matters, so economic indicators are important. The essence of schooling is who is taught what for how long and by what methods and these concerns can, following the OECD practice be called 'Flow'.

Eventually all of these aspects should have indicators. The indicators could be collected from various groups such as students, teachers, heads, school districts, states, or parents, the community, the voters. Most indicators could be an input, an output or a long-term outcome and may also be related to a process. Thus a comprehensive classification of indicators can be developed and this also will require a relational database if the measures are to be efficiently stored. Prior achievement is an excellent predictor of subsequent achievement, but each student's level of prior achievement will be partly influenced by the effectiveness of the previous stage of schooling.

One teacher's output is then another teacher's input. Teachers quite reasonably worry that if they promote high achievement at one age it may be more difficult to show high rates of progress (value added) subsequently. The introduction of baseline tests as an alternative to achievement input measures has provided an important alternative approach. The purpose of the baseline tests is not to stamp labels on students, but to predict how easy or difficult it will be to get students through the next set of examinations. What is needed for these tests, then, is typical performance, not maximum performance. In the secondary school use tape recordings for test administration so that all schools present students with the same information in the same tone of voice using exactly the same words and the same timing of each of the subtests. Old IQ tests, in contrast, are often administered in ways that are not properly standardised from school to school.

The baseline tests to obtain good predictions of subsequent achievement. The aim has been to obtain quick and efficient measures by using item formats and tasks that require many responses from the pupil that are instantly recorded and therefore add up very quickly to a good predictor of general academic performance. These tests are in some cases remarkably efficient. For example, in 20 minutes the PIPS individually administered adaptive baseline assessment for 4 and 5 year olds obtains measures that predict subsequent progress in mathematics and reading with correlations of about 0.7. At the secondary school level, the baseline test (the MidYIS test, part of the Middle Years Information System takes 45 minutes of working time and predicts subsequent achievement with correlations of about 0.7, depending upon the subject such as English or mathematics. The MidYIS test was chosen by the prestigious independent schools for a compulsory baseline.

In addition to prior achievement or baseline measures, are there other important covariates? The best source of information about relevant covariates is not what people write about, but what the data shows. Much is written, for example, of the impact of socio-economic status on achievement, but at the pupil level the correlation is generally about 0.3, thus implying that about 9 per cent of variance in the outcomes will be accounted for by knowing the socio-economic status of the student. In contrast, cognitive measures predict about 50 per cent of subsequent variation. Currently, in the Curriculum, Evaluation and Management Centre, concentrate on questionnaires to students, since education is primarily aimed at the students who are compulsory under the treatment indicator systems.

Students can tell questionnaires how much they like school, how much they like an individual subject, whether they feel safe in school, their aspirations for the future, their relationships with teachers, their health, traumas in their lives, how they are taught, and how interesting they find each subject, etc., etc. For children in their first year at school also ask teachers to rate the children's attention, impulsivity and activity levels. Certainly, when schools first join an indicator system, they can feel quite overwhelmed by the amount of data that is returned from a fully developed system. For schools in the first few years of participation 'Keep it simple, stupid' might be a good motto, especially as there is evidence that giving people too much data is de-motivating. Another wide variety of systems of indicators that involve paper- or computer-based tests, as well as 'basic' or 'extended' versions, the latter including hundreds of variables.

The system that will involve on-line administration of data collection and permit matrix sampling and the inclusion of choice, by students or other respondents to questionnaires, of the domains in which they would like to express their views and opinions. This will need close attention to the reliability of the data collected. Thus the matrix sampling will use scales as the unit of sampling rather than items. Having decided on how to measure the outcomes that matter, one is not finished with the creation of indicators. Just as prior achievement predicts subsequent achievement, so prior attitudes will predict subsequent attitudes, and in order to compare like with like need to use regression analyses and look at the residuals. The prediction appears not to be so strong as in the cognitive area, perhaps due to less reliable measures, but about 25 percent of the variance of final attitudes in secondary schools is usually predictable from knowing intake attitudes.

An indicator system consisting of dependent variables with appropriate covariates is a complete indicator system. However, an indicator system is only a step along the way to trying to understand what works, and how schooling can be improved.

Consequently, some of the indicator systems include process variables such as descriptions of methods of teaching and learning for which students in the 16-18 age range report the frequency of use. Process indicators serve to generate hypotheses and most importantly, they stimulate discussion of teaching methods among staff in schools and as such are valuable.

The cognitive data collection is standardised so that the same procedures are followed in every school. This standardisation of data collection is important in collecting data that can be validly compared from school to school. A particular threat to the validity of attitude data could arise from demand characteristics.

If students are being asked if they like the school and whether they get on well with teachers yet teachers are looking over students' shoulders, or if the students feel that their questionnaires will be scrutinised by teachers, then the situation becomes subject to possible pressures and influences that could inhibit honest responding.

In the secondary school projects, the tape recording that administers the cognitive test introduces the questionnaire part of the data collection by noting that if there is anything they don't understand they should not raise their hand and ask questions because the teacher cannot come to their desk to help them, since the teacher will be staying at the front of the class in order to avoid seeing the responses on any of the questionnaires. Of course this procedure requires that students can read the questionnaires and this may not always be the case.

The creation of a monitoring system involves a great many decisions and, as a system grows and there is feedback from the users of the system, there is a need to be responsive and flexible whilst holding firm to fundamental principles. In developing an on-entry assessment for 4-5 year olds the intention was that the data would be kept until the children reached the first statutory assessment three years later. But many reception class teachers suggested that

The use of a standardised multiple choice measure of reading comprehension, for example, is not likely to be fair to schools since teachers may not be able to influence reading comprehension skills once students can read. In other words, there is a problem of lack of sensitivity to instruction.

The matching of data from different sources can only be efficiently done by the use of unique identifiers. These preferably should be identifiers containing check digits and the computing facilities to make sure that no identifier is mis-entered. Einstein said that everything should be as simple as possible, but no simpler. This is a wise, but very challenging, piece of advice.

One cannot know how simple a data analysis can be until one has done both simple and complicated analyses and compared the results with representative sets of real data so that one is looking not only at theoretical models but also at actual magnitudes. The same data sets using ordinary least squares and multilevel models, and found, as we had found previously, that the average residuals indicating the so-called 'value added' scores for departments or schools, correlated at worst 0.93, and more usually higher, up to 0.99 on the two analyses. Thus it was possible to have the data valid and 'readily understood' by using simple regression.

The multi-level analysis, requiring special software and a postgraduate course in statistical analysis, was in contrast to the ordinary least squares analysis that could be taught in primary schools. In developing countires, the ordinary least squares analysis can certainly be presented to schools so that most members of staff understand the analysis and can use software to re-analyse data as necessary. This accessibility of the data along with the atmosphere of joint investigation (distributed research) probably helped to encourage acceptance of the indicator systems, unlike the situation that sadly seems to have arisen in Tennessee where a highly ambitious, yearly multi-level analysis was tracking students and teachers.

The development of multilevel modelling or hierarchical linear models is admirable, provides efficient calculations and rather different error terms, but to use these procedures in day to day indicator system work is likely to lead to less acceptance of the analysis by teachers. Moreover, it is somewhat akin to applying a correction for relativity when considering the momentum of a moving train: theoretically correct, but in scientific terms, an ill-advised tendency to over-precision.

Having thus confused the data, sophisticated multilevel models were applied to find that there were differential slopes, i.e. slopes that differed for high and low ability intakes. It was even suggested that teachers may be to blame for concentrating on some groups more than others. This was poor data interpretation since a confound (different subjects with different regression lines) was being attributed to teachers' actions without any corroborating evidence. The presentation of data needs to change according to the experience of the school.

A school just beginning to get feedback data needs a few clear diagrams and a telephone helpline in case of questions. Schools that have become used to receiving data and have, despite some initial rejection from some departments found it to be useful and credible, start to make more and more use of the data. It therefore becomes valuable to them to have the data provided in Excel spreadsheets, possibly with pre-programmed macros, or in specially prepared software that allows them to undertake procedures such as separating out teaching groups, aggregating by curriculum area, dropping students who have missed substantial amounts of schooling, and adding students for whom data was missing. Increasingly, as move from paper-based feedback to sending disks we provide instant feedback.

Eventually, with tight encryption techniques this will be directly over the internet. It has been important, for example, that baseline tests are not seen as predicting exact outcomes. Fifty per cent of the variation in outcomes is predictable but that means that 50 per cent is not. This problem was confronted very early in that schools were in some cases preventing students from taking advanced mathematics had they not received a C grade or higher in earlier mathematics courses. When data from a large number of schools was available, in some of which students had been allowed to take the advanced course even having not done well earlier, it was possible to present what we now call 'Chances graphs'.

This empirical distribution has great credibility with teachers and students. It is data that actually happened and if it happened once it can happen again. Thus, the low-achieving student is encouraged to recognise that many low achieving students from the previous year well exceeded the average predicted grade for that starting point. By representing their 'chances', remove the opposition rightly felt to labelling students with single predicted grades and provide actual data that is motivating for students. Compliance with freedom of information legislation and other relevant laws may require that considerable amounts of data are published.

The issue as to what should be published is taken up later since it raises ethical issues. Let it just be acknowledged here that there are issues regarding the reporting unit but also the problem arises that the vocabulary of research includes words that raise anxieties such as: 'negative', 'below average' and 'regression'. Tymms has suggested that a drift in standards seems to be characteristic in national tests in English primary schools.

The reasons for this are connected with the practice of piloting items and setting their difficulty from the results on students who knew they were simply taking an exercise. This 'adrenaline-free' un-prepared testing situation might produce lower performance that would then serve as the benchmark against which the exams were calibrated the following year. Taken under genuine examination conditions, with revision time having been invested and the adrenaline flowing, students might well be producing much better results than those calibrated. Hence the unconscious drift in 'standards'. It is an unusual teacher-training course that prepares teachers for the kind of information that is now available in England through professional monitoring systems. And yet the information is now seen as vital to many educational professionals. In the course of setting up the CEM Centre projects' sessions to explain the feedback and to discuss the implications. Further, many courses have been run locally for schools to understand and use the data.

The enormous need for in-service work is an essential part of any monitoring system and that the extent of the need for conferences and workshops often only becomes apparent as the project starts running. A school may implement an innovation and the indicator suggests worse results. But perhaps the results would have been even worse without the innovation. If instead of this year by year indicator monitoring, if a school joined with 20 other schools and a random 10 implemented one innovation and the other random half implemented a different innovation, all schools would receive 20 years of data in one year. By adopting the methods of science, learning is speeded up and made more reliable. Epidemiology and clinical trials both have their virtues, but the clinical trials are necessary to establish sound evidence as to what works. That concept applies in education as in medicine and the term 'evidence-based' is now becoming popular.

As 'value-added' became the popular word for residuals, evidence-based may become the popular word for experiments. A major ethical imperative is to do good rather than to do harm. At the very least we might try to observe the Hippocratic oath and 'at least do no harm'.

Evidence of the likely impact of indicator systems on participating schools will be considered including the small number of controlled trials that exist. In addition to this question about the overall impact of indicators there are numerous ethical issues to be addressed that arise in the course of running indicator systems. The effect of the randomly assigned feedback was measured not against no feedback but against already substantial feedback, so to expect any further improvement was perhaps optimistic.

Nevertheless as a result of giving classroom by classroom analyses to the teachers concerned, rather than simply departmental data from which this information could be extracted. In the Years Late Secondary Information System, a list of under-aspiring students is produced by combining students' intentions regarding continuing in education with their baseline scores. Many schools given the list of under-aspiring students set up mentoring sessions or special monitoring. Unfortunately, good intentions do not guarantee good outcomes.

Aware of the ethical responsibility not to have teachers wasting their time and in order to avoid harming students, they obtained permission from some schools to only feed back to them a random half of the list of their under-aspiring students. In following up these schools and comparing the outcomes of the named under-aspirers versus the unnamed under-aspirers, actually have found more differences in favour of the unnamed group than the named group. Only 15 schools were involved in this first experiment, but it calls into question many facile beliefs about how achievement can be improved. The findings are challenging and the experiment is being repeated with thirty schools. It illustrates how an indicator system can move the profession forward to proper experimentation.

The resistance to a National Curriculum in the U.S. has contributed to the slow development of curriculum-embedded, high-stakes, authentic tests. In England, where external curriculum-embedded assessments have been used for decades and school performance tables are published using raw results, moves have been made towards value added systems. These will increase the high stakes nature of the external examinations and, at the same time, government pressure on the Qualifications and Curriculum Authority has led to a reduction from seven independent examination boards to three conglomerates of the former boards.

Furthermore there has been a reduction in the number of syllabuses on offer for secondary schools. Meanwhile in primary schools, a single National Curriculum has been imposed and all primary students sit the same tests designed to the same syllabuses at the ages of 7, 11 and 14 years. The specification of a National Curriculum concentrating on particular subjects and the publication of these data has put schools under pressure to drop attention to such areas as the fine arts, the performing arts, and physical education, and to concentrate on those indicators that are published. All schools are forced to do the same curriculum unless exemptions are granted. This restriction and concentration certainly represents a downgrading of the professional status of teachers who can now make few important decisions, and it may contribute to declining levels of satisfaction of teachers. At the very least there should be various curricula available to be chosen, as was the case for decades for teachers of students aged 16 and 18 years.

Thus, a teacher who preferred to teach physical geography rather than economic geography could find a syllabus in which the proportion was attractive for that teacher. Another reason for maintaining choice and diversity in syllabuses is that in the entire population a much broader range of skills is thereby likely to be developed. Choice and diversity also keep the examination boards in competition and this ought to lead to an improvement in the quality of the service that they provide. Unfortunately, since they have a virtual monopoly endowed by government approval, it will not be likely that examination boards drop their poor practice unless required to do so. Examples of poor practice from examination boards are leaving the names of students and their schools on the examination paper when it is being assessed.

The name of the pupil and the school will often contain clear evidence regarding the pupil's gender, ethnicity, social class and religion. There may be differences between groups, but ethnicity is very poorly defined; socio-economic status is not well-measured; and neither of these variables, is alterable by the school. Religion is perhaps an alterable variable, but Catholic schools are doing better than Protestant schools. The habit of analysing by these unalterable variables may simply be a result of the pressure to produce academic papers, whether they contribute to practical or theoretical developments or not. Given a body of data it is easy to break it down by these categories, and report the differences.

The fact that it leads nowhere has not been a major consideration in social science research. The fact that such analyses perpetuate stereotyping should also be a matter of ethical concern. That these correlational analyses do not promote the search for strong evidence as to what works, is certainly a matter for ethical concern. Attention should be directed towards alterable variables rather than unalterable categories into which human beings are grouped, which is the first step to stereotyping. These analyses become particularly a matter of concern when teachers are presumed to be somehow to blame for the 'under-achievement' of boys at the age of 16 as compared with the achievement of girls. Group differences make catchy headlines in the newspapers. While there may sometimes be a need to track group differences, there is a more important need to educate users of data about the size of the effects being studied and what is known about altering the situation.

At the secondary level the damaging and unethical impact is a concentration on D students because the reporting line is the percentage of students getting Grade C or above. Time, effort and money have been spent on D students to the neglect of more able and less able students. If, on the other hand, an average points score is used as the outcome measure, the implication is to work with each pupil to obtain their maximum performance. In England, official bodies such as the Office for Standards in Education, lacking pupil level value added measures, compare schools with 'similar' schools.

The classification of 'similar' is usually made on the basis of the percent of students receiving free school meals. However, two schools can both have 20 per cent of students receiving free school meals but otherwise have quite different profiles. For example, one may have a larger proportion of children who also come from schools with very high levels of achievement. Such a school benchmarked against a school with the same percent of free school meals will look very good at the expense of the other school, but the comparison is spurious. Such benchmarking is an inadequate way of making comparisons.

The only fair comparisons are with similar students in other schools. It is certainly not ethical to make unfair comparisons which in some cases carry financial consequences for the institution concerned and can lead to job losses and demoralisation. Indeed, to take a most extreme and serious consequence, Ofsted inspectors rely on poor benchmarking data and also sit in classrooms judging teachers. In short, whole school indicators should be avoided because the evidence is that there is more variation within a single school than is generally found between schools. Furthermore, the use of whole school indicators encourages the rank ordering of schools and the public is not prepared to interpret rank orders adequately. Very small differences in the indicator can move a school through many positions in a rank ordering in the middle of a distribution. If indicators were published for each teacher, this would be tantamount to doing personnel work in public and would be unacceptable. And yet data cannot be withheld from the public unreasonably, so some compromise is needed: not whole school indicators and not individual teacher indicators.

In small schools there may be no distinction between the indicators for a curriculum area and for a teacher. There needs to be some restriction put on the size of sample that can be reported publicly. The CEM Centre is developing these indicators for the provision of data at the LEA10/School District level as opposed to individual school level, where the data is presented department by department for affective and cognitive indicators, and student by student in the cognitive area. Within the individual school, further analyses can be undertaken to obtain data teacher by teacher. Mistaken beliefs about the nature of the physical world have no influence on the physical world, but distortions of beliefs about the social world can have an impact.

One of the distortions promulgated by those seeking to implement performance related pay is that pay is the great motivator. This is only a hypothesis, and before huge amounts of money go into implementing performance related pay systems, they should be put to an experimental test in which some schools get performance related pay and other schools get equivalent money to spend as they wish. The negative influences of performance related pay are potentially the destruction of team work, the demoralisation of those who do not get a performance pay rise, the corruption of data due to the chance to make financial gain from 'good' exam results, and the message sent to students that teachers work for pay: not for their love of the subject, not for their concern for their students, but for pay.

Indicator systems, feasible because of computers, may make the public sector, and in particular public sector management, a fascinating exercise in applied social science. Finally social scientists may have some responsibility for more than arguments and papers. The actions of managers and administrators should be guided by social science findings. They can study their success in applying the findings by watching the indicators as business managers watch the bottom line or the share price. Perhaps indeed the pensions of Chief Education Officers could be tied to the long-term outcomes of the students who are in their care for about 15,000 hours of compulsory treatment.

The New Frontiers, New Technologies, New Pedagogies research project is a preliminary investigation of the ways in which information and communication technology are internationalising education in, and the socio-cultural implications of these developments. In the digital age, educational materials, whether supplemental course materials or whole online courses, are able to transcend geographical barriers. The frontiers of higher education institutions are no longer defined by commuting distances or national boundaries. Instead, their reach is now more fluid, and is increasingly shaped by the local availability of communications technologies, language skills, commonalities of interest and un-met demand in far off places. Informational and communication technologies are transforming the ways in which teachers teach and students learn. An insight into the issues that arise at the intersection of these changes, when new frontiers, new technologies and new pedagogies meet. Focusing on developments in Singapore, Malaysia and Vietnam, it explores some of the sociocultural implications of the internationalisation that results from the use of new technologies in higher education.

The project was funded by Telstra Australia and carried out by the Monash Centre for Research in International Education. It is intended to form a basis for discussion in the field and to assist in planning future research projects on the specific issues identified and to inform the development of more culturally reflexive uses of educational technologies in international contexts.

The use of educational technology is significantly altering access to higher education. New technologies are lessening geographical barriers to education. Individuals and institutions with access to the Internet have an enormous volume of educational materials at their disposal, regardless of their physical location. However, such access comes at a price, and the need for expensive hardware, software and telecommunications poses a serious financial barrier for much of the population of the region.

Academics in poor countries such as Vietnam are beginning to obtain Internet access, which allows them to keep up to date with international developments in the field, access publications and maintain international networks of colleagues. This requirement is increasing infrastructure costs for educational institutions, which is particularly difficult for public institutions in poor countries. This also creates new barriers to entry for prospective students, who are increasingly required to have independent access to computer equipment and Internet access. The geographical centre-periphery divide in education is slowly being replaced by a digital divide between those who can afford to participate in global information networks and those who cannot.

The use of information and communication technologies in education is expanding access to information, educational products and whole courses, which are coming to form a globalised information network. Access to these technologies is a precondition for participation in a global information society. Clearly, individuals and institutions that are able to access and participated in these global networks are at an advantage. However, there are, of course, huge disparities in access to information and communications technologies. In recent years, inequalities in access to new information and communications technologies have become increasingly apparent.

On a global scale, the cosmopolitanism of the wealthy is in stark contrast to the localism of the poor. With economic globalisation, increasingly the wealthy have ready access to global communications media, work for companies with branches in many countries, have colleagues and clients from different cultural backgrounds, travel regularly for business and pleasure, and generally think, feel and act transnationally. The groups which are 'information rich' in the sense that they have ready access to information and communications technology, also possess a worldview that is disembedded enough from the particularities of local conditions to allow them to traverse the cultural differences of a global arena with relative ease. In wealthier societies, such as Australia, the United States and Singapore, a large proportion of the population have access to such networks.

Public education systems in these countries are connected to global flows of information, albeit with inferior machines and lower bandwidth than the private education sector. In poorer countries, much smaller segments of the popular are able to participate. Public education systems are stretched providing more basic services across the country, while private education institutions offer those who can afford it an entry point into the global information society.

The United States have detailed the extent of inequalities in access to computers and the Internet in that country. Even within wealthy societies such as the United States, there is a clear relationship between socioeconomic status, computer ownership and Internet access. This is not to imply that one can draw a neat line between those with computers and online and those without computers and offline. Nevertheless, whether socioeconomic status is measured according to income, race or educational attainment, the same patterns appear-socially advantaged groups are also technologically advantaged. This is to be expected, but the implications of this distribution for the equity and access to online education, and for the character of the emerging markets in educational services have been largely ignored by educational institutions.

The American College Board concludes that 'the result of the new technologies may be to deepen the divide between educational haves and have-nots, and that the marketplace alone will not fix the problem. Public policy must intervene to narrow the 'digital divide' between whites and minorities, the wealthy and the less advantaged.' These inequalities are not likely to be addressed by the market because educational providers are currently competing to attract those students who can afford the technology and enrolment fees to their new courses.

International Disparities in Access to Educational Technology: On an international level, the inequalities are starker, as are the implications. Within a nation, governments can be persuaded that they have a responsibility to ensure fairer access to new media in education. For example, in the United States the Clinton government has taken steps to provide financial aid to ensure public access to groups who cannot afford to privately acquire the technology. In addition to egalitarian concerns, there is a strong national economic imperative driving this effort to provide broad access to learning technology.

Similar policies have been adopted by most wealthy nations, as much out of eagerness to universalise the reach of emerging technologies, expand their high-tech industries and train a large high-tech labour force as out of a concern with educational equality. In the international arena, however, there are no equivalent transnational entities that have the ability to redress inequalities in access to technology to provide wider access to the fruits of the Information Age. Much of the world's population do not have access to the most basic communication technologies, such as postal services and telephones, either because these are not available, not reliable or are prohibitively expensive.

To give some indication of the rate of growth, the largest Internet Service Provider, the Vietnam Datacommunication Company, has over 18,000 subscribers, of which 7,733 joined in the first half of 1999. Significantly, foreigners hold around one third of Internet accounts in Vietnam, while comprising a tiny fraction of the population. Government agencies and business enterprises hold one quarter of all accounts and individuals hold the remainder. Many institutional subscribers have many individual users. At the other end of the spectrum, Singapore has the highest standard of living in South East Asia. The government of Singapore is looking to make the country a global hub for e-commerce as a way to maintain economic growth in the wake of the Asian financial crisis.

The government estimated in 1998 that e-commerce transactions in Singapore would total USD150 million by the end of that year. In recent years there has been considerable government investment in technology infrastructure. In a recent survey of IT infrastructure investment in 55 countries, Singapore was ranked fourth in the world, behind the United States, Sweden and Finland. Singapore had 394,000 dial-up Internet subscribers in 1998, or around 10% of the population. Other estimates put total Internet access (dial-up, work and school) at 17 percent of the population in 1998 but these figures are increasing rapidly. In early 2000, the Singapore government announced a three-year initiative intended to make the country one of the top five information societies in the world, in terms of rates of Internet use and home PC ownership. These will be coordinated by the Infocomm Development Authority and include such measures as providing free e-mail address and Web pages for all citizens over five years of age and distributing 30,000 used computers with software, modems and free Internet access to low-income households. Such measures are explicitly intended to overcome the digital divide and have the potential to significantly reduce barriers to access for poor students. Singapore has long been using educational technology.

Since independence in 1965, educational television has been used to support classroom teaching. In response to the current national IT agenda, the Ministry of Education has developed an IT Masterplan, a comprehensive strategy that aims to integrate information technology throughout the educational system.

In recent years, educational institutions' spending on information and communications technology has increased dramatically around the world. Within developed societies like the United States, wealthier educational institutions are making greatest use of new media while poorer ones lag behind. While wealthier institutions in developed countries are using ICTs for course delivery, flexibility and interaction at a distance, in poorer institutions in developing countries, computers are still primarily used for teaching computer science and computer literacy. The public universities in Vietnam are the most poorly resourced of the institutions visited for this study. When viewed in historical context, however, the facilities are improving dramatically.

Staff who studied overseas return and teach students how to use the Internet and e-mail. The university is beginning to put content on to the Web, but only a few subjects are using the Web so far. Curriculum has changed in IT courses because lecturers have incorporated elements from course descriptions and lecture notes found on the Web. Students access to information is changing rapidly, especially in IT courses. First-year IT students are now required to do some research using online resources and new subjects being developed use the Internet more than existing ones. Theses submitted in the past year commonly include URLs in bibliography, and all theses submitted at HCMUT are now available online.

When the University first began to gain access to the Internet between 1995 and 1997, it was only available to academic staff members in the faculty of information technology. Even this restricted access was very costly to the institution, whose 64 Kbps bandwidth Internet access cost more then the combined salaries of the 40 academic staff in the IT Faculty. In 1998, the IT faculty developed a network connecting 14 higher education institutions in Ho Chi Minh City. These institutions now have a 256 Kbps bandwidth connection to the Internet through the network. Now, all staff and students in Ho Chi Minh City University of Technology and these other institutions have freely available Internet access. In contrast, the better-resourced private institutions in Vietnam, such as the

Asian Institute of Technology Centre in Vietnam (AITCV) use technology more extensively, but are out of reach of most students.

The majority of students at such private institutions rely on financial support from outside, which the institution tries to organise through grants from governments and corporations. Some bigger corporations that are in need of human resource fund scholarships to AITCV. As one lecturer noted, 'from the student's perspective the AITCV education is quite expensive, compared to the income level. So, more or less, people are expecting that they'll get a scholarship otherwise they won't be able to attend.' AITCV's ability to provide computer labs and Internet access in a poor country like Vietnam is dependent upon such support from international corporations and foreign governments.

Public universities in Malaysia have access to more resources than their Vietnamese equivalents but use educational technologies to a much lesser extent than the new Malaysian private universities. Public universities are focusing their energies on providing adequate computer laboratories. Enrolments at public universities in Malaysia have increased dramatically in recent years, due both to the financial crisis, which has prevented some students from studying overseas, and the Malaysian government's commitment to increase the proportion of the population in higher education. Between 1997 and 1999, the annual intake of the country's eight public universities increased from 45,000 to 84,000 students. This is a dramatic change in enrolments that, of itself, would put great pressure on any institution.

The crisis in pubic universities has been compounded by severe funding cuts. As a result, facilities in public universities are stretched at present and there is little resources available for investment in educational technology. These institutions cannot expect that their students are able to afford their own hardware. While PC ownership in Malaysia is currently restricted to the middle-class, there is a sense that computers and Internet access are becoming more affordable for most Malaysians. As one lecturer told us, at this point PC ownership becomes a question of priorities for many people.

The Internet allows for far more constant and ongoing relationships to be established between lecturers and researchers in different countries. In academia, the Internet has become a necessity for inclusion and participation in contemporary global networks. As the management and production of information becomes ever more central to contemporary capitalism, the divide between inclusion and exclusion in the global flows of information become more crucial.

Many academics in South East Asia are only slowly gaining entry to these networks, as the infrastructure is put in place and as the content of online academic interchange becomes less centred on activities in the United States. While most academics in Malaysia now have Internet connections, very few academics in Vietnam do, and these tend to be foreign nationals working in transnational institutions or ICT specialists working in computer science departments in public institutions. Universities have always been relatively internationalised workplaces, and many academic staff will have studied or worked in another country at some stage in their career.

In developing countries, it is common for a majority of academics to have received a large part of their education in developed countries. Many of the lecturers in the universities visited were educated in American and British Universities. As one lecturer in a Malaysian university explained, lecturers bring back what they have learnt in these countries and adapt it to local conditions. As well as bringing back knowledge from abroad which is then adapted to local conditions, this experience creates international linkages which the lecturers continue to develop upon their return.

International postgraduate study-Masters and Doctoral programs-which many lecturers in Malaysia, Singapore and Vietnam have experienced, often establishes ongoing research, publishing and teaching connections. Opportunities for international colleagues to meet face-to-face are infrequent, and in the past, such networks were largely maintained by letter-writing and occasional phone calls. Now, e-mail has allowed these international collaborations to be maintained on a day-to-day basis much more easily. Internet access is helping Vietnamese universities participate in global academic networks. In the past lecturers would bring back suitcases full of books on their return to Vietnam. Now they order books and download articles online.

The IT department subscribes online to The American Computer Magazine and IEEE International Electronic Engineering. They now have faster access to international information technology developments. Staff now obtain international scholarship and grant information online and can apply for these directly. In past students and academics had to rely on the government to organise these. They have established international relationships with particular lecturers overseas who organise funding and exchanges. At a private transnational provider in Vietnam, like AIT, the communications infrastructure now means that they are as connected to global networks as any other institution in the world.

Educational providers must now decide whether they will require their students to provide their own computer and Internet access. Many universities in the most technologically advanced societies now require their students to provide their own a computer and Internet access, and this is also beginning to be a requirement in private universities in Malaysia. Public distance education providers in South East Asia cannot expect their students to have access to computers and the Internet. The Hanoi Open University, for example, estimates that only 10 per cent of their students have PCs. While distance education in Australia and other developed societies has usually required students to provide their own equipment, in South East Asia distance education has relied on study centres to provide various facilities and face-to-face teaching. The GNP per capita in Ho Chi Minh City is only a little more than US$1000 per year. The GNP in Hanoi is about US$800. This makes computer equipment very expensive. Connection fees for the Internet are very high in comparison with other countries. Internet fees, like international telephony and postage rates, are very expensive by local standards. In 1999, Internet access and installation charges were cut by up to 50 percent on 1998 prices. There are different rates for government officials and general users.

Two Malaysian private universities that were visited in this study-the International Medical University and UNITAR-are strongly encouraging their students to purchase personal computers. UNITAR has its own IT shop that sells desktop computers and notebooks at special prices for UNITAR students through a deal between the institution and a manufacturer. The university provides finance so that students can purchase a PC with a small deposit and regular monthly payments. Because UNITAR's viability is reliant on students owning computers, it wants to ensure there are minimal barriers to its students owning PCs. UNITAR argues that the money students save in commuting costs and lower fees should be put towards purchasing a PC. IMU is also entering into an agreement with a hardware supplier to decrease costs to its students. It is planning to move to a new building in which it will provide numerous Internet access points for notebook computers rather than traditional computer labs.

From September 1999, new students must provide their own notebook computer. UTUM would also like to see their students migrate onto the net, but considers that this is not a realistic expectation of all students in the short term both due to financial constraints and poor telecommunications infrastructure in some places. However, the university believes that nearly all students at UTUM-which is a private university that specialises in technology courses-already have access to the net. Likewise, Monash University Malaysia estimates that 80 per cent of its Malaysian students have computers at home. The level technology infrastructure at these institutions seems comparable to most Australian universities.

Across South East Asia, governments have encouraged public universities to use distance education to deliver low-cost mass education. Distance education providers such as Universitas Terbuka in Indonesia, Universiti Sains Malaysia and Hanoi Open University have expanded access to higher education for students in outlying areas and for working adults. These institutions are slowly integrating new technologies into teaching and learning, but are hampered by their students' lack of access to computer equipment and because they lack the significant funds required for such innovation. Meanwhile, new privately-owned entrants into the distance education market such as UNITAR are capitalising on the promise of online education, painting themselves as virtual universities. Distance education can be offered with varying levels of student support.

In most cases, printed learning materials and text books are sent to the students. Increasingly, CD-ROMs, videos and the World Wide Web are being used to supplement these printed resources. When discussing distance education internationally, it is important to distinguish between 'remotely-supported' and 'locally-supported' distance education. Remotely-supported distance education is delivered to students who study independently and have little face-to-face contact with teaching staff and other students. This is common in Australia and in some other Western countries but rare in South East Asia. Much more common is locally-supported distance education, in which a local study centre provides various services to students, from tutorial support to library facilities. This may involve short-term visits by lecturers or tutors from a central campus or ongoing teaching from locally recruited staff who are able to contextualise centrally-produced teaching materials.

Most transnational distance education providers contract local partners to provide a range of services to students. Increasingly, institutions are providing students with access to tutors via the Internet, using e-mail, discussion forums and on-line tutorials. The three distance education providers visited-University Sains Malaysia, Hanoi Open University and TMC-all used local study centres to provide the hardware required by students at these locations rather than requiring students to have such equipment at home. A similar situation exists in Hong Kong, where distance education students are heavily reliant on computer facilities and workspaces provided by the institution.

Virtual Universities

The term 'virtual university' is usually reserved for institutions that have no campus and teach students exclusively by distance mode using educational technologies. This is perhaps the most intensive application of educational technologies into higher education, evidenced in the United States by universities such as Jones International University. In a technical sense, relying on Internet-based communication allows the institution to operate globally. In the earlier print/post phase of remotely-supported distance education, most students tended to live near the institution, and almost entirely within the same country. Internationalisation was difficult due to the cost, slowness and unreliability of international communications. By using e-mail and the Web, it is now possible for prospective students to choose from a wide range of courses offered by providers based in many different nations. However, in practice, online universities appear to draw most of their students from within their home country. A number of online universities have begun to market themselves internationally, including Jones International and the University of Southern Queensland.

Two institutions in the countries visited refer to themselves as virtual universities. The differences between them offer some indication of the ways in which this organisational form may be applied in South East Asia. Universiti Tun Abdul Razak (UNITAR) UNITAR is a private university in Malaysia founded in 1998 that set out to be a 'virtual' university with no physical campus, relying entirely on technologically-mediated communications. When the university was first proposed, the Malaysia Education Minister expressed concern about the lack of socialisation in remotely-supported distance education. In short, UNITAR was told: 'no socialisation, no education, no license, no operation'. In response, the virtual university model was altered, requiring compulsory attendance at local study centres in all subjects. In the first semester, attendance is required for 22 hours per subject and in subsequent semesters students must attend eight hours of classes per subject. UNITAR has had to establish a network of local learning centres, which students can attend for classes, interaction, exams and access to computers and support. These are very similar to the learning centres of established distance education providers, but with more reliance on educational technologies.

Due to the cost and unreliability of dial-up Internet connections in Malaysia, which were then prone to drop-outs and low bandwidth, UNITAR decided to distribute teaching materials to students on CD-ROMs. Students are required to go online to access the library, complete administrative tasks, participate in forums and tutorials. UNITAR established a courseware team consisting of 120 instructional designers, multimedia programmers, graphic designers and audio-visual producers. They work with lecturers and module writers, most of whom are employed on contract. UNITAR's online content is primarily text-based, including answers to common questions from students, which are compiled into a FAQ (frequently asked questions) list. Threaded discussion forums display only the last week's messages, encouraging students to read and respond regularly. Virtual tutorials are held once or twice each month, using chat, a shared whiteboard and Real Audio. UNITAR has a virtual library (as well as a small physical library on their KL campus) which holds 3,000 titles, mainly online journals. UNITAR responds to students requests and complaints through a call centre. This forwards queries on to the appropriate person by e-mail, and they should respond within 24 hours.

The university prides itself on making use of academic staff time more efficiently than other tertiary institutions by minimizing research activities and standardizing course content to minimise differences between lecturing staff. Lecturers are supposed to respond to student inquiries within 24 hours, and if the student receives no response within 48 hours, the lecturer's supervisor is notified. UNITAR intends to launch campuses in Singapore and in the south of the Philippines, and later in several Middle-Eastern countries. Their international activities also extend to providing focusing on educational technology solutions and consultancy services for the region.

The intent to work with schools, universities and virtual learning providers, both in content development and course delivery. TMC is part owner of a Singapore-based online education company, CyberCampus 21, which hosts online courses and provides related technical and educational services. These services include providing hardware, software and support services to both educational providers and users. CyberCampus 21 currently offers an online course that is taught by TMC and a Diploma in Business Administration and Marketing that is validated by Staffordshire University on a pilot run basis. They also offer two short courses called Servesafe Food Safety Program Writing Right: An Introductory Course to the Basics of Writing Well. TMC sees the online study option provided by CyberCampus 21 as one of a range of different delivery options, which their students can choose between. TMC plan to use CyberCampus 21 to offer a range of international courses in much the same way as they offer distance education courses. Online content would be provided by the international university and TMC would provide local marketing, administration, face-to-face teaching and student support.

These two institutions provide examples of two different types of 'virtual' university. UNITAR operates in a similar way to existing universities, developing and teaching its own courses, but the majority of its teaching and learning is done through computers. CyberCampus 21, by contrast, does not develop its own content but operates as a hosting service for the online components of distance education courses developed by other institutions. While all the distance education providers visited in the course of this study were moving to incorporate educational technology, none were moving away from also providing face-to-face teaching and support to students. There appeared to be no significant demand for remotely supported distance education.

As in other parts of the world, online courses seem to be most popular with working adults seeking postgraduate qualifications, especially in business and information technology. For undergraduate students, the lack of on-campus socialisation appears to be a significant disincentive.

The ability to access the Internet on campus has the potential to lift students out of a local face-to-face context and connect them with a global informational sphere. In this way, educational technologies are globalising the production and consumption of information, so that the same types of information are increasingly available to university lecturers and students anywhere in the wired world. At the same time, however, educational technologies appear to be speeding up the homogenisation of knowledge production and dissemination around the world, resulting in the devaluation of local cultures and local knowledges. Among the educators interviewed in this study, the Internet was widely seen as promoting the standardisation of curriculum on a global scale. These educators considered themselves adept at taking what was locally useful from the proliferation of online materials. These lecturers play a significant role in mediating between the producers and users of online materials, framing and interpreting the content to make it useful for their students.

On an international level, the connection of higher education institutions to the Internet furthers the standardisation of knowledge, teaching and learning. While educational technology may provide students with a larger number of online courses to choose from, it is likely that all these choices will become increasingly similar over time. In the world of networked computing, the forces of institutional isomorphism are amplified greatly.' Isomorphism here refers to the tendency of institutions to become increasingly similar through imitatation of each others' ideas, practices and organisational structures. The used of information and communication technologies in education has enhances these processes in several ways:

— The management of different institutions and different parts of the same institution must be standardised in order to be integrated into overarching computerised networks.

— The trend towards modularity, whereby students can combine subjects offered by different providers to constitute a degree, is fuelled by the increased availability of information about courses and the trend towards distance delivery. In order to respond to governments' and students' desires for greater inter-institutional mobility, universities are under pressure to standardise offerings in line with other providers.

— Greater interaction and cooperation between educators around the globe may result in less diversity in their teaching, research and publishing rather than more.

— The standardisation of computerised systems and software allows for much greater portability of educational materials, resulting in global markets for educational texts, courseware applications and multimedia programs. For example, electronic journals and online book purchasing are fuelling of the globalisation of academic publishing.

Because of the dominance of the English language in the digital realm, educational technologies put additional pressure on those aiming to maintain linguistic diversity in education. English language skills become increasingly important for students, and cultural producers in English-speaking countries have a rapidly increasing audience around the globe.

Globalisation of Knowledge

Universities have long seen science and technology as universal, culturally neutral forms of knowledge. These disciplines have been taught globally with little regard for local differences. Through the spread of Western education around the world, these forms of knowledge have become globally dominant while local knowledge, skills and cultures are often overlooked. Some writers draw attention to the ways in which the dominant forms of Western science have appropriated elements of knowledge systems from around the globe and combined them to develop a coherent world-view. In this way, science can be de-Westernised, and made more relevant to non-Western students by teaching about the diverse cultural roots of science. This does not seem to be occurring widely in practice, and the tendency is more commonly for local knowledges to be treated as inferior to bodies of knowledge imported from the most technologically advanced post-industrial societies.

While science and technology education are perhaps the most globalised, the internationalisation of other disciplines is also occurring. Monash University Malaysia began operation offering the more 'generic' courses-engineering, IT and business programs-which have been adapted only minimally for offshore delivery. In any discipline, there are aspects of the curriculum that are able to be transported more readily than others. While the theoretical foundations of many social science subjects can be taught transnationally, the empirical content of humanities and social science subjects usually reflects the social environment in which these courses are taught to a far greater degree than the sciences, business and technology subjects.

And they could apply that to here. While the specific content of such courses may vary according to the local social context, it is likely that similar theoretical approaches will guide knowledge production and teaching in very different societies. There was general agreement amongst participants in this study that 'the influence of context differs from one discipline to another', as one interviewee put it.

Vocational disciplines are increasingly having global appeal as certain types of work become globally standardised. With the globalisation of capitalism, systems of production, consumption, communications and transportation are becoming increasingly standardised around the globe, making globalised training possible in those areas of life which have become most standardised. The more the process of economic globalization deepens, the more the inter-penetration of networks of production and management expands across borders, and the closer become the links between the conditions of the labor force in different countries, placed at different levels of wages and social protection, but decreasingly distinct in terms of skills and technology.' For example, the skills required to make hamburgers, fix Toyotas or use Microsoft Word do not differ markedly from one country to another.

Technological globalisation has also facilitated the standardisation of tertiary education in a similar way, for example in dentistry, engineering, computer science, business administration (witness the international success of the MBA) and many other technologies. The most internationally adaptable areas are those characterised by 'skills and concepts which are readily translatable across countries and cultures, a strong vocational emphasis, high student and/or industry demand for tailored and flexibly delivered programs and strong industry pressure for standardisation of content across institutions.'

Transnational education, in which the institution based in a different country to its students, offers insights into the curricular issues that all tertiary education institutions will increasingly have to face in the near future. As educational materials and whole courses of study prepared in one country are used more often and more routinely by students in another part of the world, many practical issues will arise. The detail of these will vary from case to case and there is no point in trying to pre-empt them here. However, a general sketch of the responses of transnational educators is a useful starting point. Business education and computing are the most common disciplines in international trade in education.

The portability of these disciplines coincides with high demand for these skills around the world. The Internet is now essential to the operation of offshore campuses and other forms of transnational education such as international distance education. Transnational delivery usually requires that curriculum is standardised across numerous campuses located in different countries and regions, for a number of reasons:

1. Institutions achieve lower costs per student by taking advantage of the economies of scale that derive from using the same course materials (whether distributed in print, video, CD-ROM or online) for a large

number of students even though they are in different locations.

2. Accreditation by host countries often requires that the course to be delivered offshore is equivalent or identical to that delivered in the home country.

3. Consistency across campuses and between partner institutions allows students to move between campuses while maintaining the continuity of their course with full course credits.

Some students at the Asian Institute of Technology in Hanoi (AITCV) see an international postgraduate course as a stepping stone to employment in an international corporation. Salaries in international corporations are much higher than in government organisations in Vietnam, that students expect that 'if they are accepted for AITCV then they can get good jobs in joint-venture companies.' As long as international education improves students' value in the labour market, questions about the cultural and regional biases of content do not seem to concern those involved. Transnational courses are sometimes tailored to local conditions as required, but usually only minimal modifications are made, mainly in terms of content and assignment questions.

International education providers increasingly need to bridge the divide between globally- and locally-relevant education. Employers around the world now look for graduates with a balance of universal and specific knowledge, who understand local conditions but are able to work in internationalised contexts.

The Asian Institute of Technology (AIT) is an international institution based in Bangkok. It was established over 40 as the South East Asian Treaty Organisation Graduate School of Engineering to serve the educational needs of the South East Asian region and it continues to be funded by many governments and foundations. It now has faculty from more than 25 countries and students from more than 40 countries. AIT has two centres in Vietnam. The AIT Centre Vietnam, located in Hanoi, was established in 1993, as the institution's first branch outside Bangkok. It provides postgraduate education, short-term training courses, language training. Vietnamese students constitute the largest group of foreign students at AIT in Bangkok. The Hanoi centre was established to provide a lower-cost alternative for Vietnamese graduate students, enabling them to complete most of their degree in Vietnam.

More recently, the Swiss-AIT-Vietnam Management Development Programme has been established at the Ho Chi Minh City University of Technology. Jointly funded by the Swiss and Vietnamese governments, this centre delivers a graduate diploma programme in Management Development to Vietnamese business lecturers from local universities and working executives. It also provides management training and support to Vietnamese companies that are in the process of restructuring prior to privatization. In the past, AIT's campus in Vietnam relied heavily on fax communications with Bangkok. Staff now use e-mail and the Web extensively to keep in touch with international colleagues and to remain informed about developments outside Vietnam.

Students regularly use online resources and this differentiates them from the public education sector in Vietnam. According to one AITCV lecturer, 'It is a big difference between the international education system and the local Vietnamese universities. They are still closed. Students have the means to access the Internet every day.' AIT 'use the net very aggressively and in a lot of the courses they are also given references to the Web sites. They also do project work using data on the net.' However, as in most educational institutions, the Internet has so far had a much greater impact on communications between lecturers than it has on teaching.

2

Technology in Teacher Education

Teacher professional development is absolutely essential if technology provided to schools is to be used effectively. Simply put, spending scarce resources on informational technology hardware and software without financing teacher professional development as well is wasteful. Experience around the world in developing, industrialized, and information-based countries has shown that teacher training in the use and application of technology is the key determining factor for improved student performance (in terms of both knowledge acquisition and skills development enabled by technology). Educational technology is not, and never will be, transformative on its own—it requires teachers who can integrate technology into the curriculum and use it to improve student learning.

In other words, computers can not replace teachers—teachers are the key to whether technology is used appropriately and effectively. Designing and implementing successful teacher professional development programs in the application of technology is neither easy nor inexpensive. There are more cases of inadequate and ineffective training programmes than there are success stories. Moreover, success stories are not automatically transferable to other situations, and the total body of experience and knowledge in this field is in its infancy. While some people may know more than others in this area, there are few if any true "experts." This calls for humility, innovation, a willingness to fail, ongoing evaluation, sharing of both positive and negative experiences, and constant revision of teacher professional development programmes related to technology.

Even if students could learn independently how to use technology to enhance their learning and skills development, with little or no involvement from their teachers, they are highly unlikely to have those opportunities if teachers do not let them have access to technology. Teachers remain the gatekeepers for students' access to educational opportunities afforded by technology: they cannot and should not be ignored. Moreover, providing technical skills training to teachers in the use of technology is not enough. Teachers also need professional development in the pedagogical application of those skills to improve teaching and learning.

Traditional one-time teacher training workshops have not been effective in helping teachers to feel comfortable using technology or to integrate it successfully into their teaching. Instead, a new paradigm is emerging that replaces training with lifelong professional preparedness and development of teachers. This approach includes at least three dimensions:

— Initial preparation/training (preservice) that provides teachers with a solid foundation of knowledge;

competency in teaching, classroom management, and organization skills; mastery of the subject matter they will teach; and proficiency in using a variety of educational resources, including technology.

— Workshops, seminars, and short courses (inservice) that offer structured opportunities for acquisition of new teaching skills and subject matter knowledge, as well as skills development in the use of technology in the classroom, that are government-certified and linked to teachers' professional career development.

— Ongoing pedagogical and technical support for teachers as they address their daily challenges and responsibilities.

While technology increases teachers' training and professional development needs, it also offers part of the solution. Information and communication technologies (ICTs) can improve preservice teacher training by providing access to more and better educational resources, offering multimedia simulations of good teaching practice, catalyzing teacher-to-trainee collaboration, and increasing productivity of noninstructional tasks. ICTs also can enable inservice teacher professional development at a distance, asynchronous learning, and individualized training opportunities.

Finally, ICTs can overcome teachers' isolation, breaking down their classroom walls and connecting them to colleagues, mentors, curriculum experts, and the global teacher community. As has been pointed out elsewhere in this book, technology and teacher professional development in its use is best introduced in the context of broader educational reform, which embraces a shift away from teacher-centered, lecture-based instruction toward student-centered, interactive, constructivist learning. This has consequences for reform of curricula, examinations, provision of educational resources, and teachers' professional development. Indeed, one of the most exciting aspects of information and communication technology is its role as a catalyst for such educational reform. The specific content of such programs is then discussed, after which the issue of teachers' motivation and incentives to participate in professional development programs related to technology is addressed.

The importance of training additional school community members is stressed, and recommendations are offered for overcoming the persistent problem of insufficient funding for teacher professional development. Next, the potential of technology as a medium for delivering teacher professional development programs is examined, followed by a discussion of future trends in teacher professional development.

Finally, because most of this chapter is directed at educational policy makers designing teacher professional development programs, a series of recommendations is provided specifically for teachers considering professional development programs in the use of technology.

Most teachers want to learn to use educational technology effectively, but they lack the conceptual framework, time, computer access, and support necessary to do so. A well-planned, ongoing professional development program, grounded in a theoretical model, linked to curricular objectives, incorporating formative evaluation activities, and sustained by sufficient financial and staff support is essential if teachers are to use technology effectively to improve student learning.

When designing or implementing any teacher professional development program for technology, it is important to situate that program within the context of a theoretical framework for adult learning. Teacher professional development in the use of technology should be designed and implemented to move teachers (and, eventually, students) toward the right-hand end of this continuum. This framework emphasizes the potential of Web-based instruction to contribute to pedagogical reform, rather than technology's rich multimedia features or its ability to access information resources around the world. Stated more simply, technology can promote effective instruction that is more student-centered, interdisciplinary, more closely related to real-life events and processes, and adaptive to individual learning styles. Such instruction encourages development of higher-order thinking and information-reasoning skills (rather than memorization of facts) among students, and socially constructed (collaborative) learning, all of which are increasingly required in today's knowledge-based global economy. This potential of technology to improve instruction needs to be integrated into the design and delivery of teacher professional development programs in the use of technology.

Perhaps most important for the purpose of teachers' professional development, technology implies a shift in the teacher's role from being the sole source of knowledge and instruction to being a facilitator of students' learning, which is acquired from many sources. This is often referred to as a shift from being "the sage on the stage to the guide on the side." Again, teacher professional development for ICTs needs to incorporate and model this shift. Failure to incorporate these 10 dimensions of interactive learning into teacher professional development programs in the use and integration of technology will cripple the potential of technology to improve teaching and learning. This implies that teacher professional development in the use of technology should embody and model the forms of pedagogy that teachers can use in their classrooms. For example, these training programs should accomplish the following:

— Empower teachers to develop their knowledge and skills actively and experientially, in a variety of learning environments, both individual and collaborative.

— Include a variety of learning strategies, encompassing direct instruction, deduction, discussion, drill and practice, deduction, induction, and sharing.

— Aim at higher-order thinking skills.

— Provide an authentic learning environment so that teachers engage in concrete tasks within realistic scenarios.

— Emphasize ways that technology can facilitate and enhance teachers' professional lives.

— Encourage teachers to be mentors, tutors, and guides of the students' learning process (rather than simple presenters of knowledge and information).

— Develop teachers' skills in learning how to learn

— Promote cooperative and collaborative learning.

— Be sensitive to the culture and diversity of teachers as learners, using a multifaceted approach to respond to different learning styles, opportunities, environments, and starting points.

— Enable learning independent of time and place.

More concretely, this means that teacher professional development in the use of technology needs to combine lecture/ presentation modalities with small-group and plenary discussion, individual and collaborative activities, and opportunities for teachers to reflect on their actual teaching practices and how they might do things differently with technology. Such an approach also means that learning materials need to be in several formats: print, CD-ROM, e-mail attachments, online (HTML and Java), and even DVD. It also implies a need to develop both synchronous and asynchronous modalities, so that teachers can take advantage of training opportunities when they have the time, which is not necessarily when the trainer is available.

Key to successful teacher professional development programs is a modular structure, corresponding to different levels of teacher experience and expertise using technology. Adapting materials to teachers' comfort level and starting points is essential. In this way, teachers new to technology can be exposed to the full series of professional development modules, while those further along on the learning curve can enter where their knowledge and skills stop, and help their less technology-savvy colleagues along. The basic principles of adult learning also should be incorporated into the training program. This implies that the program should be highly social and cooperative, with opportunities to share experiences and combine instruction with discussion, reflection, application, and evaluation.

In addition to these principles, technology enables an even more collaborative approach and maximizes peer-to-peer sharing of the challenges, frustrations, advantages, and successes of using technology to teach and learn. Such an approach encourages use of illuminating failures in the use of technology in the classroom as well as examples of best practice. Finally, these principles imply the need to build ongoing community and systems of support from peers, mentors, and experts. Single, "one-shot" training events that leave teachers alone afterward should be avoided.

Professional Development Programmes

This topic has been discussed at length over the last 10 years as information technology, and particularly the Internet, has been introduced into schools around the world. To begin with, designers of a teacher professional development program for use of technology need to determine current teacher competency levels in this area. The International Society for Technology in Education (ISTE) has produced a set of standards for teacher skills and knowledge in the use of technology, a useful guide for determining the content of teacher professional development programs.

The "Professional Competency Continuum," can be used to determine the skill levels of individual teachers and their professional development needs. European, Asian, and Latin American educational associations have developed similar sets of standards adapted to their educational contexts. No attempt is made here to resolve these ongoing discussions and divergent views regarding the content required for teacher professional development in the use of technology. Indeed, differing economic, social, cultural, educational, and technological realities require different approaches. That said, some minimum guidelines and suggestions for the content of teacher professional development in the use of technology are warranted. Policy makers should assume as a bare minimum requirement at least 24 hours (three full days) of teacher training in the use of technology. This includes basic operating systems (turning computers on and off, opening and closing files, etc.), word processing, and spreadsheets (particularly useful for such noninstructional tasks as grading).

Obviously, the more time allocated for this training, particularly hands-on time, the greater the mastery of these basic skills will be. Teachers should finish this basic course with at least the fundamentals necessary for them to practice and develop their skills further back in their schools. Adding another 16 hours of training and Internet access would enable teachers to access information on the Internet, do some basic lesson planning integrating technology, and exchange e-mail messages and files with colleagues and experts. With this base of 40 hours of professional development, provided the methodology of the course incorporates some of the key interactive learning principles described above, teachers should be able to begin using technology in their classrooms. Experience of the World Links program suggests that at least 80 hours of professional development are required before teachers can really begin to integrate technology into their teaching.

Additional content would include linking curricular objectives to technology-based activities, development of lesson plans and evaluation strategies that incorporate technology, construction of educational Websites, and discussion of ethical issues related to technology and education. Ideally, this is provided in various stages, allowing time for teachers to experiment with and apply their new technological skills and knowledge in the classroom before moving on to move advanced applications. This approach also allows teachers to reflect on and share their learning experience (both positive and negative) with their peers, thereby promoting the social construction of knowledge. World Links has been a pioneer in developing and delivering teacher professional development programs in the use of technology to improve teaching and learning in developing countries. It is by no means the "definitive" programme, nor is it the most easily replicated and scaled.

The complete World Links Teacher Professional Development program includes 200 hours of training, equivalent to five 40-hour weeks. This takes teachers with no prior contact with computers to full competency over a two- to three-year period. In addition to content, professional development for technology should incorporate the fundamental components that research has found to be essential, including:

— Direct connection to student learning. The goal of teacher professional development is improved student achievement.

— Hands-on technology use. This requires development of core technology competencies and skills and actual application of skills in the classroom.

— Curriculum-specific applications. To the fullest extent possible, teachers need to see a direct link between technology and the curriculum for which they are responsible.

— New roles for teachers, as facilitators and guides, not simply as lecturers or instructors.

— Active participation of teachers and collegial learning.

— Professional development as an ongoing process.

Motivation

Teachers generally are reluctant to change their teaching styles and habits; are cautious of time-consuming activities that may take away from other high-priority obligations (economic, familial, or educational); have difficulty seeing the potential payoff beforehand of this kind of training; and may feel so threatened by technology that they want to distance themselves from it rather than embrace it. Put simply, many teachers require additional motivation and incentives to participate actively in professional development activities. A brief description of some incentives (extrinsic and intrinsic) that have been used successfully in the past follows.

Certification by Ministry of Education (Extrinsic): Ministries of education should be more active in designing criteria for certifying technology-focused teacher professional development programs. They can begin by seeking examples of best practices/examples of professional development programs (domestic or international), relating training programmes to existing teacher knowledge and skill standards, and comparing programs to curricula. Then, departments of inservice training should certify the best teacher training programs and link teachers' progress in salary and grade scales to successful certification. This would send a clear message to teachers and school directors that such training is valued at the highest levels of the ministry, and that it increases teachers' incentive to actively participate.

Recognition and Time Allocation by Supervisors (Extrinsic): Teachers need to be encouraged by administrators, particularly their school directors, to participate in training activities. Administrators need to ensure that teachers have adequate time to participate, and do not have to sacrifice too much personal time to do so. From an administrative perspective, this should be viewed as an investment and a contribution to the capacity building of the country's teaching force. But, in addition to time allocation, supervisors should recognize publicly teachers who successfully complete professional development courses. This provides immediate personal reward to teachers, raises their status in the eyes of their peers, and encourages others to participate.

Reduced isolation and increased professional satisfaction (intrinsic): Many teachers lead an isolated professional existence, with little input from or collaboration with their peers or supervisors. Alone in front of a class of 25-75 students, they teach according to what they learned (both content and pedagogy) several or more years ago in a preservice teacher training institute. Learning new technological skills, especially if they include Internet and e-mail, allows teachers to break down the walls of their classroom and share lesson plans, evaluation strategies, student assessments, and even just the joys and frustrations of teaching. In other words, technology reduced their isolation and made them more excited about teaching. Sharing that experience should serve to motivate other teachers to participate in similar professional development programs.

Enhanced Productivity (Intrinsic): Technology can speed up and increase the efficiency of a range of noninstructional teacher activities such as student attendance, grading, textbook distribution, and preparation of administrative reports. It also can enhance the productivity of basic instructional tasks. More advanced applications include fast identification of educational resources (online), use of CD-ROM materials.

In fact, there is a nearly limitless range of opportunities for teachers who develop the necessary skills and knowledge in the effective use of technology in the classroom, and who have access to technology and Internet. They can:

— plan, conduct, and evaluate learning projects with colleagues and students;

— receive and provide support following courses;

— participate in (or lead) topical discussions;

— conduct and attend course activities;

— find resources, experts, and new colleagues; and

— serve as resources for other educators.

Teachers may be motivated to participate in professional development workshops in the use of technology because they see them as an opportunity to become a trainer/ mentor for other teachers. In many cases, becoming a trainer brings additional financial and professional opportunities (travel, participation conferences, publications, etc.). If the training workshops come with some form of official certification for successful completion, motivation is enhanced further.

School directors, finance officers, and other administrative personnel also need professional development in the use of technology for noninstructional purposes. Technology can improve significantly the productivity of activities related to financial management, class scheduling, personnel management, student tracking, administrative reporting, communicating with parents, etc. However, training of school directors should not be limited to noninstructional uses of technology. It is vital that school directors understand and support teachers' efforts to integrate technology into the classroom. Far too often, school directors minimize the time and effort required for teachers to develop the skills and knowledge required to use technology effectively, and, in many cases, directors actively oppose teachers' efforts to use technology in innovative ways. For this reason, it is strongly recommended that all school directors participate in introductory professional development workshops in the pedagogical application of technology. If at all possible, this should be done in collaboration with teachers, so school directors understand that technology requires us to be both learners and facilitators of the learning of others.

School directors need to see the potential of technology to be a catalyst for more effective learning. They also need to understand (and empathize with) the process and the time required to tap this potential. If this happens, they will be far more likely to encourage their teachers to participate in training workshops, allow them needed release time, and encourage them to experiment with innovative teaching practices using technology.

Parallel to, and in conjunction with, teacher professional development is the need to provide training for students in the use of technology. It is shared wisdom now that youth acquire technological skills far more quickly than adults, and they are far more likely to share their skills with their peers (either deliberately or simply through interaction). Rather than seeing this as a threat to their authority, teachers should embrace this reality and use it to their advantage. Technology training for students has a "viral" character to it in that it tends to replicate itself spontaneously and spread among other students, many of whom have extremely strong intrinsic motivation to learn new skills. This motivation is related to youth's natural affinity for new technologies, their desire to improve their academic performance for downstream educational and economic opportunities, and their understanding that these skills are increasingly demanded in their countries' labor markets. Such motivation is not often present among teachers. Technologically savvy students can help teachers use technology in the classroom in many ways, especially when collaborative, constructivist, and authentic learning strategies are used.

At a basic level, students can provide technical support in the classroom to their peers and even to the teacher in the use of software, Internet research, leadership of small groups, and even simple computer maintenance and troubleshooting of common glitches. At a more advanced level, students often have more time and desire than teachers to develop their technological skills further.

Generating parent support for technology in schools is important if technology investments are to be sustained and/or expanded. World Links' experience in more than 20 developing countries suggests that parents are often the primary source of recurrent financing for technology in schools and, actually, the most logical source from an economic perspective. This is because universal access to technology simply is not possible now (even if the hardware and software were free, a huge proportion of schools in developing countries lack the electricity and phone lines needed to use them), and those schools that meet basic technical criteria usually are located in more urban and/or middle-class socioeconomic areas.

In other words, technology can exacerbate inequity of educational and economic opportunities within a country. With their children as the direct beneficiaries of technology-enhanced learning, parents are the natural source of financial support to sustain technology at the school level. Offering training for parents in the use of technology helps them to understand its potential for their children. Consequently, such training makes them more likely to bear a portion of the financial burden and encourage their children to take advantage of these new opportunities. In addition, trained parents can become invaluable "monitors" or aides in school computer labs, either paid or volunteer. This eliminates the need to assign teachers to the computer lab during nonteaching hours, encourages greater school-community integration, and provides opportunities for students and adults to share their skills and knowledge with one another. In many cases, "champion students" can offer training to parents and other community members.

Once teachers have mastered the basics of ICTs—operating systems, word processing, and e-mail and

Internet navigation—they can use the technology to access professional development opportunities. This enables anytime, anywhere learning and overcomes the conventional limitations of face-to-face training workshops (cost, travel, accommodations, and low numbers of participants).

Models for Online Professional Development: Many different technologies have been used to support or provide teacher professional development. Often grouped under the vague heading, "distance learning," they include basic correspondence courses, broadcast television, interactive radio, and video. This section focuses on the potential of new digital technologies (the Internet, digital radio, CD-ROMs, DVDs) for teacher professional development. To begin, it is important to distinguish among different approaches or models for online professional development.

Advantages of Technology Use

The Costa Rican experience in training teachers to use technology, and using technology to train teachers, is instructive. Over the course of 12 years, more than 15,000 teachers and administrators have been trained, using both face-to-face and distance methodologies. Teachers engage in training online on their own, at their convenience, and they can do so as often and for as long as they want. Ongoing pedagogical support and teacher networking, key ingredients of effective inservice training, are facilitated by the technology. By infusing technology into the teaching and learning process, teachers' career-long professional development has become a continuous and planned process. Technology extends training into and beyond the classroom, no longer bound by fixed schedules or physical spaces for instruction (anytime, anywhere learning).

This dramatically increased Costa Rican teachers' motivation for, and participation in, professional development in the use of technology to improve teaching and learning. This potential can been seen in the evaluation of the World Links Program by SRI International, in which more than 80% of teachers surveyed reported that their attitudes about teaching improved "a lot" or "a great deal" as a result of their involvement in the program. The program offers access to technology and the Internet, teacher professional development, involvement in international telecollaborative programmes, and development of online educational content by the teachers themselves. But perhaps more important than providing additional training opportunities, the use of the Web as the training medium exposes teachers to pedagogical practices analogous to what they may do with their own students using technology.

Teachers begin to learn skills and develop new knowledge online, through interaction with instructors, mentors, peers, and subject matter experts, modeling the potential learning experience of their students after the training. More specifically, from a pedagogical perspective, teachers working together online with their instructors, peers, and experts share and collectively construct their skills and knowledge. This replaces the traditional vertical training model of trainer imparting information "down" to a teacher.

Using technology to train teachers should not be considered a panacea, however. It is very hard to implement, and the number of successful cases in developing countries is very small. Even in the United States, online teacher professional development programs experience an average dropout rate of more than 30%, in most cases because of a decline in participants' motivation or availability of time. There are a number of strategies and approaches to maintain participant motivation:

— Don't overload the course. Comprehensive coverage of every topic may not be possible or desirable. Focus on quality not quantity.
— Whenever possible, include materials and assignments that can be used in the classroom.
— Look for ways to involve trainees in course assignments.
— Encourage group work and discussion among teachers.
— Take advantage of the fact that your audience is composed of fellow educators.
— Endeavour to involve teachers in the latest research.
— Expose teachers to new educational products and teaching methods.
— Always keep teachers informed about grades, assignments, etc.
— Use teaching assistants extensively to increase personal contact.
— Clarify course requirements and grading policies.
— Expect diversity among participants in terms of both mastery of subject matter and familiarity with technology.

— Keep online conversations active and lively.

— Grade and return assignments promptly.

— Help teachers to set and adhere to a study schedule.

— Use short, open-ended responses to promote online discussion.

— Force teachers to stay together and keep up with all readings and assignments.

For some middle-income developing countries online learning is 127 already in reach because of the spread of technology in the schools and sufficient communication infrastructure. For most developing countries, however, problems of low bandwidth, telecommunications costs, limited computer access, etc., require maximum use of offline training modalities, such as CD-ROMs; use of store-and-forward e-mail for sharing documents and mentor support, video, diskettes; and even printed materials to support other technologies. This presents a paradox: Before technology can be used for teachers' professional development, teachers need face-to-face professional development in the use of technology. But experience in countries such as Chile has shown that with as little as a half-day of face-to-face training, teachers can develop enough knowledge and skills to participate successfully in technology-based distance learning activities.

Future Trends

Future trends in teacher professional development in the use of technology will be shaped by two main factors: increasing demand for teacher training and new technologies/ methodologies to enable that training.

The demand from ministries of education and teachers themselves for professional development in the use of technology is outpacing the capacity of conventional approaches, such as face-to-face training, to respond. There is a simple issue of scale as ministries of education implement nationwide educational technology programs, and the sheer numbers of teachers who need to be trained exceeds financial, human, and technical capacity to handle teacher training requirements. In addition, greater complexity and content of the training are required as the Internet and other new technologies are introduced. At the societal level, what teachers are expected to know and do is increasing every year. Teachers not only have to know their subject matter and basic pedagogy, they also are expected to model higher-order thinking processes, work in interdisciplinary teams, and demonstrate leadership and communication skills. At the same time, they are supposed to deliver better student results on standardized tests, while addressing larger societal problems.

Traditional teacher training approaches simply are not equipped to deal with all of these new expectations. By contrast, ICTs can help teachers to meet these expectations, by providing productivity tools, access to information and colleagues, and collaboration opportunities. As teachers experience these external pressures, and realize the potential of technology to help them respond, their demand for training in the use of technology will grow. Scale and complexity exacerbate the issue of teacher motivation. Ministries of education around the world are struggling for techniques and incentives to get beyond the "champion teachers" and so called early adopters to reach the average teacher. Paradoxically, there is both excess teacher demand for training (relative to capacity to provide it) and insufficient teacher demand for training (relative to the physical distribution of computer hardware in the schools).

New teacher professional development methodologies are required to address this issue of motivation. In the future, ministries of education will issue new standards for teacher competencies in the use of technology, which will affect both preservice and inservice teacher training levels. These standards are likely to be linked to official certification requirements and processes, so that education ministries can track the proportion of teachers who have the necessary skills and knowledge, and so that teachers have an incentive to participate. As the need and demand for teacher professional development increases, the key challenges will be ensuring content quality, reliable and appropriate training delivery infrastructure, follow-up support, and measurable outcomes—and all at an acceptable cost.

New Technologies and E-Learning

E-learning is a way for teachers to learn new knowledge and skills using computer network technologies. The technologies provide not just text, but also sound, video, simulations, and collaboration with other learners who may be scattered around the country or the world. Currently, most e-learning is delivered using the World Wide Web; however, future e-learning could include delivery via mobile handheld devices, cell phones, and digital video devices. The rapidly declining cost of digital video disc (DVD) production and replay offers exciting opportunities to capture the work of master teachers and trainers and share this with teachers wherever they are. Internet-enabled DVD will be available soon, so that teachers learning with a DVD will be able to access materials and resources located on the DVD itself and on the World Wide Web. A $250 DVD player linked to a computer (and perhaps an Internet connection) would bring full video and audio capabilities to professional development, in combination with community-building tools and other resources. This will open up a whole new range of visual and audio possibilities in a distance training format, which is easily scaled.

As Internet access and bandwidth improve in developing countries, additional Web-based synchronous and asynchronous teacher professional development opportunities will arise. For instance, a reliable 56 Kbps Internet connection would enable online teacher professional development that includes live voice-over-IP, file sharing, control of all participants' computer screens by the instructor-facilitator from anywhere in the world, online assessment, and many other features. The instructor-facilitator would control the microphone, be able to 'pass' it to participants when they want to ask a question or make a comment, provide individualized evaluation and support to participants, and do this with teachers located in 25 different countries simultaneously. Holding this up are basic telecommunications infrastructure, the telecommunications costs of extended online connections, and regulatory issues surrounding voice-over-IP.

E-learning is rapidly developing because of four main factors:

— gradually increasing availability of higher-speed computer networks to deliver information and services;

— recognition that teachers need to 'work smarter' with constant updating of skills;

— convenient just-in-time education for teachers; and

— cost-effective alternative to traditional classroom-based education and training.

Professional development of teachers in the use and application of educational technology should be designed and implemented as part of a broader educational reform program that, at a minimum, combines technology access with teacher professional development and local content development. No strategy that ignores any of these three elements is likely to succeed beyond superficial applications. Ideally, teachers' professional development should not be isolated from other elements of instructional and noninstructional educational environments, such as curriculum reform, physical/technological infrastructure, examinations, and research. Simply providing professional development for teachers in the use of computers and the Internet, in a situation with outdated curricula, traditional standardized test systems, and insufficient technology access, is unlikely to produce any systemic improvements in learning. In fact, the high-stakes traditional examinations system frequently operates against teachers trying to incorporate technology and encourage deeper forms of learning, which frequently are not measured by standardized tests. Teacher professional development in the use of technology to improve teaching and learning needs to be:

— multifaceted,

— modular,

— authentic,

— collaborative,

— incentivized,

— iterative and ongoing,

— allocated sufficient time and financial resources,

— cost-effective, and

— evaluated and revised.

While it is neither easy nor inexpensive to design and implement teacher professional development programs in the use of new technologies, it is an absolutely critical element of any initiative to introduce technology into schools to improve teaching and learning. Failure to invest sufficient resources in teacher training will result in failure of school-based technology initiatives, which would result in substantial wasted investment that few, if any, developing countries can afford. Success in ensuring that teachers acquire the skills and knowledge they need to use technology effectively opens the door to all kinds of new educational opportunities for both teachers and students, and downstream economic opportunities for graduating youth and their countries. It is the key to participation in the global knowledge-based economy.

3

Digital Technologies for Education

Education has always lived a tension between two functions. On the one hand education is a matter of assuring continuity, that is, passing on what is known. On the other, it is a matter of fostering creativity and change, that is, propelling learners into the unknown. Both of these functions relate equally to knowledge and attitudes, to understanding and behaviour. They are simultaneously complementary and conflictive. They touch the essence of the teaching/learning process. We want creativity, but we want it to emerge from what is known and understood. We want continuity, but when the result is lack of ability to solve problems or devise ways to improve the human condition, are dismayed.

Since education has, fortunately, come to be considered as a human right, the main instrument of delivery of basic education is the school, and the right to education is, with exceptions, perceived as a right to schooling. So the tension between continuity and change is played out in an important way in the classroom. Thus it is extended to the need to simultaneously expand access, guarantee uniform quality, and leave room for diversity of results. In the educational process, people are central. The role of teachers is always crucial. But, in each of the elements described above, the human element has limits, and other interventions need to be brought to bear strongly into the process of delivery and transformation of knowledge, and verification of results. It is the potential and role of technologies in contributing to improvement in the effectiveness and efficiency of this profoundly human exercise that this book addresses. One of the most universally recognizable and enduring human institutions is the school.

Changes in schools over time have been mainly in the logistics: physical plants, materials, and comforts or conditions of teachers and learners. In many cases, technologies have been brought in to enhance an otherwise static process. The learners gather, the teachers communicate information, the learners reproduce what they have heard and seen, and they are evaluated on their accuracy. The relevance of this process to life has been questioned often but seldom modified substantially and never system-wide. Over the past 200 years, we have tried to perfect the education services provided by schools. The education model from education for the few to education for the many; from education for limited objectives to education for expanded objectives; from the environment as the classroom to the classroom as the learning environment; from elitist endeavours to national education systems. Even technical schools have tried to replicate the workplace in the school. In this development, we were inspired and helped by the industrial age and its processes.

Schools were to a large extent modeled on factories, where cohorts and student flow evoke assembly lines, time-on-task parallels working hours, exams are designed as a form of control of the uniformity of the product, and the production function of a school takes us back to the input/output model of factory production. Despite its shortcomings, the school system has been remarkable in its contribution to the fulfillment of basic learning needs, to skill formation, to scientific progress, to reproduction of the social order and the preservation and evolution of cultures. The achievements of the last century, marvel at the extraordinary advancements in science and technology—space exploration, unraveling of the atom, genetics, organ transplant, the car, radio, television, the fax machine, the computer chip, the Internet—to name only a few.

All of this was possible because of a set of unique human features: the capacity to acquire knowledge generated by others and build on it; the ability to record one's knowledge and disseminate it to others in understandable terms; the desire to search, explore, and make sense of the universe; the urge to apply knowledge to solve day-to-day problems; and the faith that nothing is impossible or beyond the reach of the human mind. Educational institutions at all levels are the embodiment of these human features and have been at the center of human achievement in science, technology, social studies, and the humanities. They have been the arenas for the generation, advancement, and dissemination of knowledge; the training of human capital; and the engines of social and economic development.

They have excited many minds, opened new doors into the mysteries of the universe, and dared many spirits to delve into the unknown. Many have served as strongholds for the pursuit of truth and values against prevailing beliefs, prejudices, and intellectual and political tyrannies. This cannot be said of all institutions, however; many have copied the body but failed to capture the spirit. Despite the relative success of the education enterprise, the new century brings a fresh set of challenges and pressures for which educational institutions, in their present form, are not prepared. Even the best of them have served a different set of demands for a different age. These challenges in the context of the Information Age have put schools and school systems across the world under tremendous pressure to provide every classroom (if not every student) with information and communication technologies (ICTs), including computers and their accessories and connectivity to the Internet. The pressures are coming from vendors, parents, businesses, and technology advocates.

Decision makers are faced with two myths: a macro and a micro. The macro myth is that merely providing ICTs to schools transforms the learning process, and merely connecting to the Internet changes the learner's world. The micro myth is that providing technologies means acquiring computers and securing a connection to the Internet. Experience shows that effectively integrating technology into learning systems is much more complicated. It involves a rigorous analysis of educational objectives and changes, a realistic understanding of the potential of technologies, a purposeful consideration of the pre- and co-requisites of effectiveness of ICTs for education, and the prospects of this process within the dynamics of educational change and reform.

In fact, experience is proving, to our surprise, that acquiring the technologies themselves, no matter how hard and expensive, may be the easiest and cheapest element in a series of elements that ultimately could make these technologies sustainable or beneficial. This chapter is an attempt to frame the issue of ICTs for education in the context of the educational enterprises struggle to be relevant, responsive, and effective in meeting the challenges of the 21st century. To this end, the chapter draws on worldwide knowledge and experience to delineate the potentials of ICTs for education, the parameters for turning this potential into effectiveness, and the prospects of applying these capacities in different environments.

Emerging Trends in ICT and Challenges to Educational Planning

There are make two points are here:

— The speed with which the revolution in information and communication technology (ICT) has taken place is phenomenal.

— The changes the ICT revolution has wrought are not limited to one single sector of society, nor do they just add another column in the aggregate tables of macro-economists. ICT transforms all sectors of the economy. The changes have been faster, deeper, and more sweeping than anyone imagined as late as two or three decades ago—even by those who have pushed the new frontier. It also can be argued that talking about "the ICT" revolution is a misnomer; for there has not been one revolution, but five—so far.

The Computer

The first revolution started during World War II, with the first large, automatic, general electromechanical calculator. It was 50 feet long, eight feet tall, and weighed five tons. A couple of years later, ENIAC was presented in Philadelphia, based on radio tubes and practically without any internal memory, yet using 18,000 vacuum tubes and weighing 30 tons. Each time a new task was to be performed, some 6,000 switches covering three walls had to be thrown. "Computers" became a new catchword, and input-output technology graduated from punch cards to magnetic tape, faster printers, and more languages for programming. Applications also were expanded, from use in academic research to weather forecasting, from airline ticketing to accounting. This development continues; the first ICT revolution is still under way.

The PC

The second ICT revolution has its roots in the 1970s, when the first "processors on a chip" and magnetic discs were constructed. But as late as 1977, Ken Olson, the legendary president of the computer company, Digital, stated:

> "There is no reason anyone would want a computer in their home." He was definitely wrong. In the same year, Steve Jobs and Steve Wosniak started to sell their Apple II, and Bill Gates and Paul Allen had already founded a firm called Microsoft. From being an esoteric toy, the personal computer gradually became a valuable tool for word processing, accounting, and, after a while, pictures. IBM, which at first grossly underestimated the markets for the

personal computer (PC), launched its first machine under that name in 1981. Now the PC has become as widespread as the radio when our grandparents were young—indeed, as widespread as bicycles are among today's youth. This second ICT revolution continues like the first: the capacities of the machines increase, their applications expand, and the number of people who use them multiplies.

The Microprocessor

The third ICT revolution is that microprocessors have become embedded in an ever-widening range of products: the steering systems of airplanes, the control panels of hydroelectric power stations, domestic air conditioning systems, the traffic lights in our streets. Even when we do not recognize it, they have become part of our everyday lives: in video players, credit cards, remote controllers, cameras, hotel room door locks, and smart buildings. There is a microprocessor embedded in our digital scale in the bathroom. If you use an electric toothbrush, its functions are governed by some 3,000 lines of programming. Microprocessors translate bar codes into prices at the cash register, monitor electronic injection of fuel in our cars, and determine where the elevator stops in our building. An ordinary household now contains some 100 microprocessors, in everything from dishwashers to alarm systems. Microprocessor constantly expand their capacity, applications, and users.

The Internet

The fourth ICT revolution stretches back to the late 1960s, when the U.S. Department of Defense drew up guidelines for a communication network among computers (ARPANET). After a while, universities in and outside the United States were hooked up to it, and some started to use it to send messages. France developed its variant—its Minitel system—at the beginning of the 1980s, at the same time the U.S. National Science Foundation set up its own network among academic institutions that later became part of Internet. A dozen universities on the U.S. East Coast with IBM mainframes contributed with BITNET. In Europe, EARN became a network among academic institutions, while CERN in Geneva was crucial in the development of the World Wide Web, which got its name in 1990. A couple of years later, surfing on the net started, and more and more people hooked up. A PC needed a modem to use its potential fully. This fourth ICT revolution continues like the others as more and more computers are interlinked with an ever-growing number of "servers" and an expanding range of applications. Yet, the most important part of the fourth ICT revolution was this: on the computer networks engineers had constructed, users built social networks to make them useful and effective—in this case, the social superstructure built on the material basis became really super.

Wireless Links

The fifth ICT revolution was linking without lines—the new possibilities opened by mobile phones. At first, they were big and bulky. Reduction in size and weight was accompanied by expansion of reach and functions, and miniaturization was accompanied by multifunctionality. Mobile phones could be used not just for talking, but also to exchange messages, receive news or stock exchange quotes, review restaurants, or order movie tickets. Phones are no longer only for transmitting phonemes; now they can transmit written messages, pictures, and music. Linking without lines now takes place not just intercontinentally via satellites, but also via high-frequency short-range radio transmitters covering a specific area or cell (hence the name, "cellular phones") and inside buildings by "Bluetooth" and infrared light.

Impact of the ICT Revolutions

The emerging trends to make there are four general points are here:

— The speed and impact of the ICT revolutions provide modern illustrations of Says's law: Supply creates its own demand, PCs have become household appliances. When they were linked via telephone lines, they were transformed from isolated stations to nodes in networks, and their usefulness increased exponentially with each additional node. When new functions were added—access to libraries, e-mail, etc.—their value multiplied. PCs, their links, and their multiple functions were innovations that soon became necessities.

— The way the hardware of ICT was produced and operated has itself become one of the foremost expressions of globalization; components come from all continents—chips from Asia, software from America, mobile phones from Europe. Brand names have instant recognition around the world: Acer, Sony, Intel, Microsoft, and Nokia. On the other hand, satellites orbiting the globe allow for instant communication on an unprecedented scale.

The Internet also changes the ways schools work by making possible closer cooperation and interaction among them, within the same country and across continents and oceans. One example is joint "virtual projects." Likewise, parents can be kept informed via the Websites of schools—virtual PTAs, so to speak. Not only has ICT transformed the way learning institutions work, it also has changed the way we think about organized education. ICT has become a medium in the original sense of the word: something in the middle, between the substance to be learned and the student who is to master it.

— it liberates provision of education from the constraints of time and place: many courses can be accessed from more or less anywhere and at any time.

— Training can be customized, by allowing material to be adapted to individual levels and tasks to be paced according to personal progress.

But tailored capacity and development does not mean that students cannot interact—individualized does not mean isolated. To the contrary, the physical network allows students to work together, whether for mutual consultation and advice or support and encouragement. Hence, the new education technologies alter the means and modes of studying. Students can link to other students, across boundaries and across continents. Children can take part in the development of learning materials for each other in other classrooms or countries. Teachers in the remotest places can be encouraged to take part in important professional development programmes. Indeed, the whole education system can work like a neural network, where cells with synapses to other cells can fire them up.

The Internet also can become a network for altruism. Institutionally, so much on the Web is there for free and for all. A large part of the available educational resources is created by groups outside of schools and academic institutions, yet is free for all and provides excellent inputs for learning. Sometimes, such worldwide community service is well organized, such as the scanning, typing, or proofreading of classical texts that are entered on Websites open to all, or when the classification of craters on Mars is set up as voluntary work among informed amateurs linked by the Internet. Individually, some communities have experimented with tutors mentoring students from home. Such acts of generosity allow those participating in them to engage their minds and help others; it sure beats the millions of clicks wasted on solitaire.

— The development of new products and services was part of a vast distributed and yet integrated global division of labor, whether it was in the development of new for-profit products and services or the more altruistic open-source contributions from a diverse crowd of enthusiasts.

— The new links—the Internet and the World Wide Web—became the first truly dynamic and interactive network that individuals could access from all over the world. Much of what is on the Web is not mass communication in the classical sense: one source, one way, many users. It is by and for interacting people. Indeed, in many respects individuals were ahead of institutions in realizing the Web's potential. For example, music was swapped via the Internet before it became commoditized.

The ICT revolution has been very much about spotting opportunities and inviting everybody to learn to make good use of them. Indeed, the ICT revolution is perhaps above all else a revolution in learning. Individuals have seen the potential of the new tools and introduced them into their homes on a vast scale. Firms have applied them to an ever-widening range of activities: bookkeeping, production control, management, communication, marketing, and drug development. Public authorities have incorporated them into all of their activities, from vaccination programs to tracking criminals.

Since the ICT revolution is a revolution in learning, it also has transformed available technologies, the means and methods of studying, the modalities of school operations, the manner of investment and expenditure of resources, and the very way we think about what education could be and should do.

Even before the Internet became a new mode of communication, and the World Wide Web made it possible to access learning material anywhere, universities had started to use telecommunications and computers for teaching. But with the advent of the Internet and the Web, these opportunities have expanded vastly, and educational institutions have made more and more varied use of them. Course material is posted on the Web, assignments can be communicated through the net, and teachers can be accessed around the clock by the new modes of transmission. The new education programs have reached out to off-campus students, often from long distances, but they also have reached in to regular students in novel ways by providing learning materials in new forms.

Challenges to Educational Planners

The ICT revolution offers new intrinsic opportunities; it dramatically changes what can be learned and by whom as well as what can be produced and provided by whom. These potential changes, however, pose many new challenges for educational planners. These challenges can be divided into two broad types: those that pertain to equity and those that pertain to quality. But unless educational planners respond to these changes and challenges with commensurate speed, they will become, so to speak, technologically challenged.

Although in many Western countries, the majority of households have PCs linked to the Internet, considerable differences remain along regional and class lines. Several studies document that boys are more active than girls in using the new technical tools. And though schools also are increasingly well equipped and connected, standards vary within countries with educational level and type. The same applies to teacher training and skills. This raises the broader question of equity: within countries as well as between countries, particularly between the industrialized and developing world. It is true that millions of PCs are sold every year and millions gain access to the Internet.

Hence, the pressing problem for educational planners is how to reach, within a reasonable time, the needs of the majority who are poor, uneducated, and live in rural areas: how to fund, implement, and maintain the educational part of ICT networks. This question is all the more pressing because most major international teleoperators do not include sub-Saharan Africa or the remote areas of Central Asia in their business strategy plans.

Many countries have adopted ICT policies for their education systems that cover not only hardware and infrastructure, but educational materials available for schools and students as well. Such materials, increasingly available on the Internet, range from mathematics resources in Norway to lists of recommended books for California's schools. They can be accessed freely by both domestic and foreign users. In addition, many teachers and professional associations make their best work available free for anyone to use.

And this is not all. Education equals finance—public funds to be spent and private demand to be targeted. Hence ICT, and particularly the Internet, is not only an arena for altruism and experiments, but also for business, entrepreneurship, and, sometimes, exploitation. In other words, education is increasingly becoming a market, and a global one at that. In a market, there are customers and producers. And access to the production side of this market is even less equitable than access to its usage side. Some nations also actively promote programs for foreigners by distance education via the Internet. Australia is a prominent example, where services from its educational institutions have grown into a whole export industry.

This is a very interesting and, in many respects, auspicious development, but it also raises a whole range of questions for educational planners about quality, certification, and accreditation. It is notable that the World Trade Organization is considering proposals to add the import and export of higher education courses to its protocols on services marketed internationally; "education products" can then be traded as a commodity from one country to another. This development provides further opportunities for students. It releases education from national control, and it makes the market a stronger force in the globalization of education.

On the other hand, planners and officials in developing or smaller countries may face an expanding international market with powerful actors and many new ventures about which they have imperfect knowledge, exercise scant control, and have few possibilities for participation. Thus, the issue of equity pertaining to ICT has to be addressed along two dimensions:

— equitable access of students as consumers, where the poorer peoples and nations are put at a disadvantage; and

— equitable provision of content, where the poor are even worse off.

Ideally, one wishes for equal opportunity to participate. But access for different actors—both as users and producers—is weighted by their resources. Hence, initial differences are often reproduced, reinforced, and even magnified. A formidable challenge, therefore, continues to face planners of international education: how to define the problem and provide assistance for development.

As ICT is rapidly becoming an integral part of the social environment and as our jobs are being transformed rapidly into tapping on keyboards and looking at screens, traditional literacy is no longer sufficient—what could be called, "Iteracy," becomes imperative. Learning to work a PC and surfing the Internet is becoming crucial for functioning in the workplace, for effective citizenship, for entertainment, and for personal growth. With the rapid change in technology, training cannot be a one-shot affair; we have to be updated continuously to stay abreast of developments. Planning and designing educational systems so that they familiarize students with a technology that is being modified and evolving continuously is not just an intellectual challenge, it is also an economic one.

This problem is exacerbated by the fact that many vendors of new technologies are sometimes more pushers than providers, promoting solutions that have a short useful life or little compatibility with what emerge as industry standards. The history of information technology is not just a history of innovation but also a history of misguided investments. This situation applies to hardware as well as to "learning packages" and software that promise more than is delivered. What is bought is often expensive and inappropriate, resulting in costly mistakes, not just in economic terms, but in terms of time stolen from students who would have been better off using more proven methods of learning. Sometimes new solutions are pushed by politicians and ministers as well: they feel they need to prove they are "modern' by going for gadgets, but they are out of office when the negative results are in. Moreover, it takes time to discover where the potential of ICT in education can best be tapped, and as technology itself is changing, final solutions will continue to evade us.

The learning process also may be skewed in unfortunate directions. Much is made of the fact that ICT has become increasingly "interactive." Learning programs can be tailored to each student, learning at his or her own pace, and being introduced to more challenging tasks as learning proceeds. However, interaction in learning cannot be restricted to person-machine relations; person-person relations will always remain crucial. In industrialized countries, no previous generation of children has had so little contact and communication with the world of adults. Learning has become more age-graded, as has all social interaction. TV, videogames, and Internet-provided pictures and music draw the young into a more virtual world.

Hence, rather than formal education also placing students increasingly in front of a screen, planners must be concerned that students are engaged in more real than virtual interaction and connected to actual adults rather than just to their products. Children and youth need positive feedback from applets, but they also need to be seen and respected by peers and grown-ups as real people. What holds for the educational process also holds for educational content. Demand-driven education means, increasingly, education that is "just in time" and "just enough." Learning what is deemed not immediately relevant may be discarded as definitely wasted. But this concept of knowledge and skills is a perversion, even of a utilitarian justification of it. It is a perversion of the rationale for a broad liberal arts education where the goal is not just to enable one to solve a problem at hand but to develop abilities as a human being to perceive and to participate, to experience, to empathize, and to excel. But then the whole diversity of one's talents must be nurtured and developed. Education, after all, means to "lead out," within and beyond one's present confines, by bringing out latent abilities and talents.

There is another issue with demand-driven education as it is commonly practiced. The growth in knowledge does not just generate a steady stream of new facts, findings, and products—about viruses, proteins, or superconductors. It also means that older knowledge becomes superseded. For instance, it is no longer useful to know which electronic vacuum tubes could be used in a computer. But new facts and data do not only mean that knowledge may become obsolete. They also mean that certain types of established knowledge become more important.

The periodic table of chemistry is as valid at the start of the 21st century as it was at the end of the 19th. In short, there are fundamental frames of reference that are imperative for interpreting new information, for searching for new facts, and for new everyday applications. Knowledge of such valid models, concepts, and theories determines what we grasp of what is unknown. The discovery of DNA does not overthrow molecular chemistry; it extends its uses in biology. Hence, the stream of innovations and findings, more than ever, requires fundamental knowledge—i.e., systems for interpretation and reconstruction. Without familiarity with such systems of reference, the explosion of knowledge leads only to more confusion. Also, from a social point of view, it is the acquaintance with such frameworks that makes it possible to meet new challenges and that prepares us to gain insight, review the situation, and renew strategies; it was general knowledge about retrovirus that made it possible to quickly identify the cause of AIDS. Even from a purely utilitarian view, "just in time" and "just enough" knowledge is misguided.

- It takes knowledge to know what you need to know.
- Truly new insights are often the result of serendipity—the happy chance combination of seemingly unconnected ideas to a new conception. "Just in time" knowledge is, in practice, often too late, and "just enough" knowledge often makes you miss the critical piece to solve the big puzzle.

Educational planners have to consider what a well-rounded education is. The whole point of education as a common human enterprise is that no student can bring out his or her potential if left to the student's own haphazard personal search. Students have to be led out, "educated" in the original sense of the word. There are already considerable differences say, between the offerings in mathematics and history compared to those in music and physical education. Much depends on how ICT-assisted learning is done, and, as in traditional teaching, there are no fast formulas. Discovering and developing the potential of ICT will surely take time, and what we find may not be valid for all time because the context surely will change.

Technology in itself is not a panacea; uploading Web content in different subjects does not in itself result in quality teaching or effective use. Teachers have to be trained and need to feel knowledgeable and skilled—not always easy in an environment where young students are often quicker than their teachers to learn new technologies. On the other hand, the lack of willingness to mobilize the young to learn from one another—in the same way as they learn the tricks of new video games—is not only old-fashioned but even counterproductive.

Educational planners can focus no longer just on how to secure implementation; they need to arrange for continuous experimentation and innovation to learn by doing in an ever-changing environment where even what is being learned and done is changing.

There are optimistic theories about development—about a great technological leap forward or about latecomers' ability to leapfrog generations of already outdated technologies. Yet, the digital divide will be with us for years to come, and the poor will remain in the worst position for a long time, even under the most ambitious programs. Yet, perhaps the greatest divide is between the gains would all reap if all of us could use the potential of the new technologies to develop our talents in ways that could benefit us all, and the willingness of those of us who are in the rich parts of the world to enable, empower, and involve all those who are now poor, at the margins, and not connected.

There are five major trends have characterized the development of ICTs:

— Complementarity—ICTs complement, rather than replace each other. Videoconferencing and digital radio are two examples of how different technologies are associated to improve results.

— Speed of growth—ICTs have grown exponentially. In 1950, personal computers were little known or used, but within a generation, they became essential work and communication tools. The number of Internet hosts worldwide grew more than 1,100 times in eight years.

— Reduced costs—Increased use of ICTs is associated with reduced costs and improved technology. This trend is particularly felt in the computer industry, where hardware prices have fallen, despite significant increases in memory and speed. Internet access is another area where growth has been accompanied by some cost reduction.

From 1999 to 2004, the number of U.S. households online is estimated to increase by 66% (from 40.5 million to 67.1 million), but spending on access is estimated to rise only 9.2% CAGR (compound annual growth rate). Similarly, broadband Internet access is expected to increase 800%, from 2.1 million subscribers in 1999 to 18.9 million in 2004, while broadband spending will grow 527%, from US$1.1 billion to US$6.9 billion, respectively.

Simplification—ICTs strive for simplicity of use, even when the technology becomes gradually more complex. The first disk operating system- (DOS-) operated personal computers (PCs) required some training for simple before, ICT access is related positively to economic development—the higher the region's income, the greater the ICT access. But, income is not the only variable that influences access to technology. In the United States, for instance, there is a correlation between race and computer ownership or Internet access. Whites are more likely to own a computer than blacks, even when controlling for differences in education, except for those at the highest income levels.

Between December 1998 and August 2000, the gap in Internet access between black households and the national average grew from 15% to 18%; for Latino households, the gap grew from 14% to 18%. In China, significant differences exist in age and gender among Internet users—approximately 50% of Internet users are between 18 and 24 years of age and 75% are male.

A similar trend is found in Brazil, where 61% of the Internet users are male, and 56% are aged 14-24. Access to ICTs depends on three basic prerequisites: infrastructure, costs and financing mechanisms, and legal frameworks.

Infrastructure

Until recently, most information and communication

technologies depended on electric power and telephone lines. The production and consumption of energy varies broadly across countries in direct relationship with their economic tasks; however, children have no problems dealing with modern PCs. This concern with the user may explain, at least partially, the rapid popularity of the medium.

—*Problem-solving focus:* Perhaps more than any other technology, ICTs strive for efficiency: they are faster, simpler, less costly, and more productive. This search for efficiency propels ICTs to continuous improvements. Auto industries have relied on one source of fuel for the past 100 years, despite warnings ranging from potential extinction of this sole source to environmental disasters. In less than 50 years, telecommunications have experimented with simple telephone lines, fiber optic cables, satellites, and wireless technologies, and research continues.

These characteristics encourage and challenge a planning process that aims at introducing technology in education. The encouragement comes from the fact that educational agencies and countries can leapfrog from pretechnology stages (e.g., the absence of telephone lines) to state-of-the-art strategy (e.g., wireless technologies), thus bypassing less efficient and generally more expensive alternatives. The challenge is that technology planners must be creative and look toward the future to ensure they are not missing a better and less costly option.

Access to ICTs and the digital divide: Access to modern information and communication technologies varies greatly around the world. Until now, ICTs have not corrected the divide between technology—rich and technology-poor countries initiated with the Industrial Revolution. In 1999, average monthly rates for Internet access in Latin America ranged from US$81.71 in Trinidad & Tobago to US$12.75 in Peru, with a regional average at US$36.23.

As a means of mass communication, radio has many advantages: it has broad outreach, is relatively inexpensive, is easy to use, and is present in almost all households around the world. In addition, radio programs are less expensive to produce than television, videos, or computer software. Although radio lacks the visual effects of television and computers, educational programs broadcast via radio have popular appeal. Most of all, radio does not require complex infrastructures. Battery, windup, or solar-powered radios ensure transmission even where electricity is not available or dependable.

To overcome the limited and unreliable electricity supply in the region, the project staff built a structure with eight solar panels and seven deep cycle batteries. This structure provides all the lighting and power needed to operate the station during the 18-hour broadcast day. In addition, the solar installations have a life span of more than 10 years and low maintenance costs development. Developing countries tend to have lower levels of energy production, less efficient systems that produce great loses during transmission and distribution, and lower consumption levels. On average, poor countries consume 5% of the energy consumed by wealthy countries. The consumption range is wide, varying from 21KWh in Ethiopia to approximately 24,000 KWh in Norway. Availability of telephone mainlines follows similar distribution: wealthier countries—and wealthier regions within a country—have more phone lines per inhabitant than countries and regions with weaker economies.

For instance, while Switzerland has 675 mainlines per 1,000 inhabitants, Rwanda has two. Residents in the largest cities in sub-Saharan African countries are twice as likely to have telephone lines as those living elsewhere in the country. In South Asia, urban residents will be five times more likely to have telephone lines, in contrast with the European Union, where the ratio between urban and nonurban areas is approximately 1:1. Within the same world region, differences also can be significant. In Latin America and the Caribbean, for instance, Chile has 203 mainlines per 1,000 (281 in the largest city), while Haiti has eight (17 in the cities). In the Middle East, the United Arab Emirates have 389 mainlines per 1,000 (374 in the largest city), while Iraq has 31 and 75, respectively. Costs strongly influence access. Despite reduction in costs in the past decades, indicators still show significant cost differences among countries and within countries in a single region.

In sub-Saharan Africa, the average cost for a three-46 46 amount and type of information that is being exchanged electronically. A simple 2400-baud connection can only transmit about 240 characters per second of an e-mail message. Audio and video applications through the Internet require a minimum of 14.4Kbps, and videoconferencing needs 128Kbps.

The expansion of the Internet and, more recently, e-commerce created a new demand (and new solutions) for more bandwidth. The bandwidth demand between Europe and the United States is expected to grow by approximately 80% a year. In response, digital subscriber line (DSL) cable and alternative proposals are multiplying, mostly through private companies' efforts to ensure their share of a promising e-market. Between 1995 and 1997, the private circuit capacity between the United States and other OECD (Organisation for Economic Co-operation and Development) countries had a compound increase of 172% and surpassed the capacity allocated to international message services (mostly public).

Education projects may profit from this market-driven growth. In the past 10 years, wireless technologies have gained increasing acceptance among residential and business users. However, they should not be seen as the solution for all the problems with infrastructure. Start-up costs are high, and the project requires highly trained technicians; some wavebands are highly sensitive to weather conditions, thus increasing the probability of errors, and they require a high level of coordination to avoid interfering with other radio spectrum users. In places with an already well-developed network, fiber optic cables offer more transmission capacity with smaller margins of errors and at lower cost. Where the infrastructure is missing, wireless technologies may be a solution, even if only a temporary one.

Considering the speed of change in the ICTs industry, discussions on the use of ICTs for educational purposes should focus not only on the technologies available, but also on those that are in the planning stage, and should evaluate how feasible and affordable they are for each specific case.

Partnering also allows schools to share resources, including software, Internet connections, training programs, and full-time support staff, thus reducing significantly the overall cost of the project.

Many large-scale projects on the use of technology for education are financed through partnerships between governmental agencies and bilateral and international organizations, such as the U.S. Agency for International Development (USAID), the World Bank, and the United Nations Educational, Scientific and Cultural Organization (UNESCO). Within countries, projects may be financed through interdepartmental partnerships. For radio- or television-based projects, private and public broadcast organizations may provide free or reduced-cost airtime. Foundations are key providers of one-time expenses, such as upgrading hardware and software. Public-private partnerships associate the political and financial power of government with the flexibility of private enterprise.

Educational programmes using technologies require start-up investments that may challenge the limited resources of poor countries or locales. However, technologies also offer solutions that help to defray costs without jeopardizing the quality of the projects. Creativity is essential to overcome potential barriers, as shown in the following suggestions:

—*Unbundling:* Educational institutions, particularly universities, can contract out support functions that are complex, expensive, and extraneous to their main purpose. Organizations are already forming to pursue this objective. The only function of the Queensland Open Learning Network in Australia and the European Study Centres is to provide support to learners and educational institutions. The IBM Global Campus and the McGraw-Hill Learning Infrastructure, in the United States, provide consultation, project management, and technical support to educational organizations. The unbundling process enables each agency to focus on what it does best, thus increasing productivity.

—*Focus on efficiency:* If technology projects focus on where the need is greatest, the project can have the most impact. About 50% of the students in community colleges are enrolled in just 25 courses. These are the large introductory classes, generally taught by assistants. Technology projects that prioritize these courses will reach basically all students on the campus. In addition, since those courses feed other disciplines, improving their quality will result in a better foundation for more advanced courses. This strategy has the potential to reduce repetition and dropout rates, thus increasing the efficiency of the system and offsetting the costs of the project.

—*Recycling:* Computer-based projects require significant investment in hardware. In addition, the expected active life of a computer is about five years, and as the hardware industry develops more sophisticated products, the software adapts to the top-of-the-line products. Between 1998 and 2000, an estimated 70 million computers were discarded in the United States alone.

Computer recycling is an ecologically sounded alternative to this problem. A growing number of not-for-profit organizations are dedicated to the tasks of collecting, refurbishing, and finding new homes for old computers. The recycling process has been facilitated by the development of new software. For example, NewDeal provides even old PCs, such as the 386 and 486 series, with the basic features of newer hardware. The software includes a contemporary graphics interface, spreadsheet, database, word processor, e-mail, and a Web browser. It has even a point-and-click interface, like Windows 98, with two major differences: it runs on any PC, from a Pentium III model to a 286, and it costs less than US$50.

— *Collaboration:* Collaboration is key to the feasibility of many projects and can happen in different ways. For instance:

i) *Adapting existing materials:* producing programs is a major part of the fixed costs of a radio- or television-based educational project. Locating and acquiring existing programs may reduce the costs of production while maintaining the quality of the product. The scripts of the English as Second-Language radio program from an IRI project in Kenya were implemented in Lesotho with only minor editing. Similarly, the mathematics lessons developed for the radio program in Nicaragua were used in other Spanish-speaking countries with only minor adaptations.

ii) *Dividing the work:* the International Virtual Education Network (IVEN) involves a partnership among a group of Latin American countries to improve mathematics and science teaching in secondary education. The partnership will develop Internet-based modules that cover the range of topics on math and science in the two last years of secondary school. By dividing the work and expenses among all participating countries, the project becomes feasible and affordable for each individual country.

iii) *Sharing resources:* Elementary and secondary schools can ensure ongoing and affordable technical assistance for their hardware by offering internships to relevant professional schools and universities. Telecenters can provide a diversity of services to accommodate the needs of different uses. In planning a technology-mediated programme for education, attention must be paid to the laws and regulations that will affect the project, either facilitate it or create barriers to it. ICTs, with their ability to reach beyond political boundaries, defy many of the national and international legal frameworks that were created for a world with frontiers. Solutions, albeit necessary, are difficult to find and slow to implement. Proposals that have been advanced by experts include the following.

Telecommunication monopolies and restrictive regulations have been part of strategic defense programs in many countries; however, calls for deregulation and liberalization of this sector are now heard everywhere. Deregulation is expected to bring competition, thus promoting more supplies and lower prices. While protecting equal access to all must remain a central concern, there is evidence that government-controlled monopolies are not always the best answer in a fast-moving technological environment. In many countries, local education authorities are profiting from liberalization of telecommunication services by entering into agreements with private providers, many of which see agreements with community-based projects as a public relations investment that enhances the company's image and increases its local support.

Accreditation and certification must in the long run maintain confidence in educational offerings by guaranteeing their quality and the acquisition of qualifications both to individuals and to employers. Systems of accreditation developed for concrete institutions may not apply in the virtual environment. Regulations on building safety or student/ instructor ratios do not pertain to the virtual world. Credit hour is another concept that does not fit distance learning.

Created to protect students in the traditional learning environment, accreditations might become a barrier against a global education market. A student may be discouraged from taking online courses if the institution offering them is not accredited in his or her country, regardless of how prestigious the institution may be. Countries with centralized education may have an advantage in terms of recognizing credentials or facilitating transfer of credits. Decentralization, in this case, may be one more obstacle for students and institutions alike. Country, state, and local regulations can be mutually exclusive, making it cumbersome or potentially impossible to create distance-learning programs that meet the diverse requirements.

Ensuring access to technologies is just one step in the success of ICT-mediated educational projects. Securing the project's acceptance is equally important. Cultural and political factors may promote or create obstacles to the use of technology or limit its use to certain subgroups of society. Likewise, the structure and organization of local educational systems may favor integration of technology or create a technophobe atmosphere that hinders efforts to change. Overall, acceptance of technologies has not been a problem. ICTs have been well received worldwide, and it appears that the older technologies opened the door for the more recent ones. As In India, places that did not have a telephone now have Internet kiosks where families can e-mail their relatives abroad.

Radio and television are now part of the world culture. However, computer and Internet use is still dominated and controlled by a small group of predominantly wealthy, educated, urban males.

Regardless of the country, the data are very similar. Access is a key issue, but access alone does not explain the data. The elderly and women, even in urban areas, trail behind young and men in ICT use. Surveys on acceptance of computer-related technologies among these population subgroups were not found; yet, anecdotal information from the field suggests that males and females of all ages and cultural backgrounds are potentially open to technologies that improve their lives and put them in contact with the world.

The elderly Internet use among the elderly is growing. From 1999 to 2000, Internet use among North American women aged 55 and over grew by 110%, making it the subgroup with the second-largest growth in the country, just behind teenage girls. Educating the elderly is a measure of good economic and social policies. The median age of the world's population is rising, and among the elderly, the older subgroup (80 years and older) is the fastest-growing group. Medical knowledge indicates that an active life is the best protection against emotional and physical illnesses, regardless of age. Moreover, in some countries, such as those devastated by the AIDS epidemic, the elderly already are assuming the unexpected roles of principal breadwinners and caretakers of orphaned children. Preparing them for these responsibilities is essential to reduce the emotional and economic impact of changed roles. Brain research shows that aging does not affect the ability to learn, although it may require different strategies that rely less on memorization and more on problem solving and critical thinking.

These are the strategies required to learn new technologies. China is catering to its elderly population through the Universities of the Third Age (UTA). UTAs use distance learning technologies—from postal correspondence to the Internet—to reach urban and rural elderly across the country. The rapid growth of the UTAs reflects not only the large demand, but also the ability of the elderly to adjust to alternative learning environments mediated through technology.

In many developing countries, women are caught in a circle of poverty, illiteracy, and cultural traditions that function as barriers to computer-related technologies, which are expensive, literacy dependent, and defined as a male realm. The stereotypical view of computers as male tools exists even in developed countries. Research in the United States shows that girls are not expected to excel in technology and are given less encouragement to use computers or pursue a career in the field. Parents buy computer-related gifts for boys more often than for girls, and teachers in technology classes tend to give more time and assistance to boys than girls.

The fact that training generally is provided by men adds one more barrier, particularly in countries that impose limits on contact between genders. The scarcity of female role models in technology-related professions is another disincentive on a path already full of obstacles. Yet, research shows that, when girls are given the same opportunities and support provided to boys, they perform as well in technology-related projects.

Since the reasons for the problem are varied, the solutions must be multiple. Suggestions include:

— At the elementary and secondary school level—train teachers and school administrators to understand their biases in relation to girls and technology and develop strategies to overcome this bias; train female teachers as technology instructors; work with parents to encourage or support their daughters' interest in technology; encourage and support girls to participate in computer clubs and other technology-related activities.

— At the tertiary level—implement public and/or private scholarships targeted to women pursuing technology careers, and provide encouragement and support for those who are in predominantly male schools, including offering opportunities for studies abroad.

— For adult education—include female instructors in telecenters to ease women's transition into technology; educate the public to understand that technology promotes economic growth for the whole family; promote projects targeting women, since men can profit from them as well, while the reverse may not happen.

Acceptance of technology is also related to the level of political support or resistance at local and national levels. National governments have been key players in the expansion of educational projects that depend on technology. Most mega-universities have privileged access to telecommunication systems that is controlled or regulated by the government in their base country.

Measures that government can take to support and expand technology-mediated projects include:

— Invest in infrastructures.

— Review fiscal policy to favor educational and nonprofit use of technologies.

— Deregulate telecommunication monopolies while protecting educational use of telecommunications.

— Reorient funding policies to serve students, rather than institutions.

— Fund technology-mediated projects directly or encourage these projects through tax relief and other benefits.

— Fund projects that ensure access to technology for underrepresented populations.

— Promote teacher training that uses technology to familiarize teachers with these tools.

— Simplify regulations and accreditation requirements to facilitate transfer of credits across states or neighboring countries.

— Implement standards of quality for distance education courses.

— Foster progressive policies on education that encourage activities related to higher-order thinking skills rather than memorization.

Interest groups outside the educational establishment may have powerful influence on promoting or creating obstacles to the use of technology for education. Digital corporations, such as Apple, funded pioneer computer experiments in schools. Many technology giants, such as Lucent Technologies, are directly involved in providing training.

Within the education establishment, acceptance of technologies is an issue, and the expansion of distance learning institutions has been met with its share of resistance. Teachers, from basic to higher education, are essential to the success or failure of educational projects, but rarely are they involved in the planning stage of these projects. Despite all the rhetoric about modernization, teacher education programs rarely include technology as content or strategy. Graduates of most teacher training institutions have little experience in using technology and no information about how to integrate ICTs into curricula and practice. The technology is mostly seen as an add-on to traditional classroom teaching, and many times as an unfamiliar, and therefore, threatening imposition. An add-on approach inhibits the potential of the technology to improve the quality and effectiveness of education and decreases support from parents, students, and the public in general, who see technology as an expensive investment with no visible trade-off. Totally integrating use of technology into the teaching/learning process presents another challenge.

Teachers may feel they are losing control over the content of the course and the students. The path from center of instruction to facilitator requires a new paradigm, and many teachers are not prepared to make the change. Distance learning stretches the paradigm even further. The personal interaction that had been the basis of the teacher-learner society is no longer there. For students, the distance learning approach may be seen as depriving them from contact with the teacher—although many times, this contact in a campus university is a myth as a weekly class for 300 or more students jams into an auditorium. For instructors, distance education requires greater preparation for planning and production, extra training in technology, and less control over students' reactions to the material. It also brings concerns over job security. For schools and universities, distance education requires greater investment, including preparation and delivery of materials ahead of class time, ensuring office hours for student queries related to academic content and to technology issues, access to library and other resources, and an efficient system of tutoring and support. Yet, changes in the student population and their interests, employee demand for training and retraining of the workforce, and market pressures will be the determining forces in the expansion of technology-mediated learning.

In other words, the boundary-less characteristic of distance education seems to equally threaten the existence of national cultures and of a universal culture shared by all educated human beings. These are epistemological concerns that raise a new perspective on the social role of education in the years to come. Few studies on cultural and political influences over the acceptance or rejection of technology-mediated educational projects are available. More is known about teachers' reaction toward technology. In general, this reaction moves from resistance to acceptance as soon as the value of technology is understood.

Educational materials for ICTs are easy to find; the challenge is to find good materials that incorporate sound pedagogical strategies and use the potential of the adopted technology fully. Two basic criteria that must be taken into account when evaluating an education material are quality and viability. The quality of a product can be judged through direct examination, references, reviews, testimonials from users, or awards. Viability is related to the useful life of the product. A good product that maintains its usefulness for a long period will produce reasonable returns on the investment. This is easier when the potential number of users is large, posing particular challenges for groups limited in size by language, culture, or educational needs.

Many organizations have developed criteria to evaluate contentware, particularly software, but each educational system should define its own standards to reflect the project's objectives and curricular requirements and the specific needs of students and teachers. The use of commercially developed material saves time and avoids production costs, but also has disadvantages, such as:

— The material may not meet local curriculum standards or educational objectives;

— The content will reflect the ideologies and lifestyles of the producing country, generally the United States;

— For non-English-speaking countries, language is a barrier; and

— Most of all, product licensing and royalties can erase the savings realized at the production stage.

Sharing materials among countries is a better option when agreements on royalties can be reached. Sharing is easier for countries with the same language and similar customs, and for topics that have a more universal nature, such as mathematics and science. Translations, albeit expensive, may prove cost-effective, and software translators are becoming common, although the quality of their work is still questionable. Partnerships with universities, broadcasting, or software companies offer another prospect for obtaining educational materials that are customized to a country's reality and needs. Open-source software is a response from the digital community to the increased control of technology-related property by large corporations. Not all open-source programs are free, although most require only nominal fees or voluntary contributions.

The movement regulates itself through ethical norms that ensure recognition to the author and protect the integrity of the product, while encouraging new product development. Since the program codes are open to reviews and improvements from a number of experts, the quality of open-source software tends to be superior to that of commercial products. In addition, the programmes can be customised to the user's specific needs. For developing countries, the open-source movement makes it easier to obtain high-quality products, avoid the costs of commercial software, and develop an expert workforce. Rather than buying a package of commercial software for each of its computers, a school district in a developed country can hire a skilled programmer to configure an open-source material to the district's specific needs and duplicate it for as many computers as necessary. The district will have a quality product for less cost, without infringing on national or international laws. In addition, the process stimulates growth of local programmers, supported by an international network of experts.

Training for educators generally is limited to use of specific programs or software packages; beyond that, educators are on their own. No institution will train educators to be technology experts, and few will provide them with a broad understanding of the requirements and potential of the technologies they will be using. Improvisation is currently the norm in this field. However, countries should look more carefully at technology for education. The development of specialists in educational material reduces dependency on imported products, while increasing the probability that the language and content of the products are appropriate for the users. It also creates a workforce that brings a fresh perspective to a field controlled by a small group of producers—a competitive advantage in the global market of educational services. Over time, investments in this workforce will bring large returns. Education services constitute the fifth largest service export in the United States. In 1997 alone, the United States spent US$26 billion on education-related goods and services, including textbooks and supplementary materials (US$11.6 billion), technology (US$4.8 billion), and testing/test preparation (US$3 billion).

The growth of educational expenditures is not limited to the United States. Worldwide sales of educational software to schools in 2000 were estimated to be US$4.1 billion, with another US$2.1 billion sold to consumer markets outside schools. By 2009, the education market is projected to grow to US$200 million in India, US$580 million in South Africa, and US$1.7 billion in China.

Capturing this market is a tempting possibility for many commercial enterprises, particularly if developing countries choose to remain buyers rather than producers. Currently, few tertiary institutions and projects seek to create this cadre of specialists. The International Virtual Education Network (IVEN) for the Enhancement of Science and Mathematics Education in Latin America is forming teams of content experts, graphic designers, instructional designers, and programmers to develop educational material focused on mathematics and science for secondary education. A few universities in Latin America offer courses to train distance learning educators, such as the Universidade de Brasilia or the Universidad Abierta de Venezuela. This is a new frontier that merits careful attention and support from educators and decision makers.

Let us examine the role of ICTs in the context of the global opportunities and challenges confronting the design, delivery, and administration of education to meet the diverse needs, clients, demands, goals, and objectives of nations and communities—particularly during a period of transition of societies and economies from an industrial base to one that is knowledge- and information-centered.

Cynics would claim:

> Some nations may decide to invest in technology for education for the "glitz factor": the technology is there; it is fashionable to have the latest and the best, and it gives a sense of progress to use state-of-art-technology. This can be described as the technology for its own sake rationale. Other nations may base their investment decisions on the genuine case for improving the efficiency of their education systems or for some other benefits intrinsic to education. For instance, databases and computerized records in education systems have clear advantages and benefits. This is the "technology for educational benefits" rationale. A third rationale may be external to education and concerned with developing skills for the labor market.

A different view of the use of ICTs is Bill Gates's, who says:

> "Students can look at their grades and even turn in their homework over the Web. Teachers hold online discussion groups. Students e-mail friends and family as naturally as they call them. Students are the ultimate knowledge workers. Their 'job' is to learn and explore and find unexpected relationships between things."

In between cynicism and optimism, one government took the view that it is "fully committed to ensuring that all schools and teachers are in a position to deploy new information and communication technologies [ICTs] to raise educational standards to enhance learning and to prepare young people with the ICT skills they will need in society and at work in the twenty-first century."

Functional illiterates

Apart from about 900 million illiterates globally, there are almost half as many adults who cannot cope with the demands of daily life because they lack literacy.

Annually, in Asia alone, about 15 million people become disabled as a result of war, diseases, accidents, and malnutrition. Their major hope for self-improvement lies in obtaining needed skills. Long-term unemployment is a debilitating pathology; training people in such situations poses special challenges to delivery and pedagogy.

Out-of-work youth, especially boys: This group is highly vulnerable to socially disruptive behaviours. Youth need vocational training, including apprenticeship and self-education, to be part of a productive economy.

Women and girls: In many parts of the world, women and girls still find themselves marginalized in education and training; ways may have to be found to circumvent the social, cultural, and economic impediments they face.

— *Refugees, recent immigrants:* Today, roughly 125 million people live outside their countries of origin, and this number is ever increasing. This flow of people for political, social, or economic purposes is not expected to slow down. To help these people resettle, educational programs, language teaching,

> and training for social and job skills must be designed and delivered. In contrast with this escalating demand is the lack of preparedness of a vast majority of our education systems to deal even with existing demand, under circumstances that, in the words of one activist group, "violate the rights of children" through "dilapidated schools, inadequate facilities, poorly trained and under trained teachers, inadequate supplies of learning materials, irrelevant curricula, disregard for minority cultures and languages, gender bias and instructional methods which undermine, rather than nourish the potential of children."

World over, the arrival of newer technologies certainly seems to have stimulated a resurgence of interest in diversifying methods of knowledge delivery. Almost daily, yet another Web-based course becomes available from one university or another. Smart schools are springing all over the richer world, and virtual learning, online learning, and other, newer forms of educational delivery are becoming part of the educational jargon of the new century. Even before the arrival of the newer technologies, institutions such as the this question let us look at the challenges confronting countries worldwide.

Many factors are contributing to the changing educational culture, the most important of which are economic, social, and technological forces. These forces are worldwide in scope and power, and have had a profound impact on business practices, manufacturing processes, financial services, government policies, and, more recently, teaching practices and learning behaviours. It would not be an exaggeration to say that as we embark on a new century, we are also moving irrevocably in the direction of changing the way we think about information, knowledge, and learning. Individuals and governments are beginning to recognize that planning for 'competitive advantage' will require a labor force that has literacy and numeracy skills beyond three to six years of primary schooling (the current situation in most industrialized and newly industrializing countries, and even grimmer in developing nations).

Globally, some 2 billion people who are in today's workforce will continue to be there well into the first quarter of this century. Their knowledge and skills will need continuous renewal. Added to this, we need 1 billion more young children and adults who will require initial education and training. The challenge of providing education and training to a huge and diverse population with a variety of learning goals and styles, at an acceptable cost, will require new forms of global educational delivery. Notwithstanding the skepticism of many in the academic community, recent reports from agencies such as UNESCO, the Organisation for Economic Cooperation and Development, and the World Bank seem to say as much. In some ways, the emergence of new technologies may have something to do with the push to make drastic changes in the nature of the learning environment.

There is also a change in the nature of those requiring education and training. Communities no longer are content (nor should they be) to limit access to education and training to the fortunate few who are able; literate; live in urban communities; have access to communications, infrastructure, and classrooms; are knowledgeable about learning opportunities and options; and have the resources to pay for them. At the same time, variations of these modern technologies allow educators to tailor content to suit a narrow local audience to respond to individual learning needs. Satellite, community, and Internet-based (through telecenters) delivery of content all enrich the environment for learning.

Agriculture, farming, health, market conditions, maternal care, and reproductive sciences all being delivered today through ICTs. Local community radio and telecenter facilities are extremely versatile tools and are used effectively and imaginatively around the world today. A key feature of the modern global society is the 'primacy associated with the exchange over computer-communication networks of intangibles such as knowledge, ideas and intelligence, rather than tangible goods that have long been the basis of human interaction'.

It is also becoming fairly clear that the power of the computer chip will continue to increase while the cost of building it decreases; bandwidths will broaden and convergence heighten; and the penetration of the Internet will continue to rise while the lack of connectivity drops. Acquisition of up-to-date knowledge, skills, and education will determine the success of individuals and democratic societies both economically and socially. It is not surprising, therefore, that an ever-increasing number of countries wish to see their citizens technologically literate. From "telecenters" to "smart schools" the push to make every child computer-, Internet-, and Web-savvy has fast become an overriding concern for education ministers of developed and developing countries.

Illiteracy

Despite the knowledge explosion and advances in information and technologies, in many countries, there are significant numbers of people who cannot read, let alone enjoy the benefits of a technological society. Every country in the world has committed to decreasing drastically the number of illiterate citizens. Mass media, especially print, radio, and, to a certain extent, television, has played a significant role in adult literacy programs. In some parts of the world, newer technologies have been applied, albeit in a modest way. An increase in the use of ICTs seems to be constrained by financial resources, shortage of literacy workers skilled in using technologies, and lack of technical support for a well-functioning technology environment.

However, ongoing developments using online resources to train literacy workers and Correspondence School of New Zealand; the National Open School of India; the Open Universities of Sri Lanka, Hong Kong, and the UKOU; and the Indira Gandhi National Open University of India were providing good-quality, mass, flexible, and lower-cost education for remote learners from basic to university-level education using the older analog technologies of print, audio, video, and radio and television.

The experience and successes of these institutions around the world are testimony to the effectiveness of technologies to reach individuals and large communities simultaneously. They have transformed the delivery of education and, in the process, also transformed the business of education. In addition, full-time study within the timetabled constraints of the classrooms is only accessible to a few; for many who wish to study, learning has to occur at a time and place of their choice. The growth of open schools, polytechnics, and universities, as well as the numerous suppliers of correspondence and online education, are all manifestations of peoples' desire to learn at their own convenience rather than at an institution's call.

It is estimated that the total amount of information doubles every four to five years. Stated in another way, the total of information available to an undergraduate in 1997 was less than 1% of what will be available to a student in 2050. Teachers have to become expert in helping learners to navigate through this sea of information rather than attempt to be effective transformers of that information into knowledge for the learners. Students must be trained to bring about this transformation, during and beyond the school years. ICTs are crucial in coping with the explosion of knowledge over the lifetime of the learner; otherwise, peoples knowledge becomes obsolete, and countries become marginalized.

The structure and content of learning activities should equip all children, youth, and adults with the knowledge, skills, values, and attitudes they need to survive, to improve their quality of life, to empower them to participate fully and responsibly in the life of their communities and nations. This education also should help them to initiate and adapt to the changing circumstances of their environment, and to continue learning according to their individual needs and interests. Clearly, any strategy to engage all citizens in lifelong learning will require application of technologies, especially mass media. For the first time in the history of humankind, communication technologies enable us to reach millions of people across will include ordinary people, along with thousands of college and university students.

Planning for effective use of ICTs in education necessitates understanding the potential of technology to meet different educational objectives and, consequently, deciding which of these objectives to pursue. This decision affects the choice of technologies and the modalities of use. This section structures the discussion around four objectives that may be enhanced by ICTs:

— expanding access to all levels of education;

— improving the quality of education;

— enhancing lifelong learning; and

— facilitating nonformal education.

Expanding Access for All to All Levels of Education: In most developing countries, full-time study within the time constraints of classrooms is only accessible to a few; for many who wish to study, learning will have to take place at a time and location of their choice. In addition, access to learning for those living in remote areas and those who are marginalized, isolated, or disadvantaged has to be sought vigorously as nations respond to the declaration made at Dakar in 2000. Either synchronously or asynchronously, barriers such as time, distance, and social and cultural constraints must be overcome. At the same time, rapid changes taking place in the workplace will require training to be delivered quickly. Such create literacy products seem to demonstrate significant results. ICTs have the potential to:

— reduce the isolation many adult literacy providers and students experience;

— facilitate communication among staff and students within and between programs;

— increase access to high-quality materials and emerging research;

— streamline administrative and reporting processes; and

— help to provide the delivery vehicle for innovative instructional and staff development approaches.

On one hand, the planet is filled with highly skilled and talented people in all fields of human endeavor. On the other, critics of global educational systems constantly bemoan the fact that, by and large, the academic talent needed in schools, colleges, and universities to enhance the quality of the learning environment beyond perceived levels of mediocrity is in short supply. We need excellence in our teaching, and we need to obtain our teachers from the best in the local community and distribute them to the whole learning community.

As a policy consideration, the application of ICTs to enhance access to learning must receive the highest priority. ICTs in their many forms have been applied in a variety of contexts, including:

Provisions have to be made to reach, in particular, children in many parts of the developing world where formal schooling is likely to account for less than 1,000 days in their entire lifetime. Fewer than half of primary-school-age children actually are enrolled in school, and more than two-thirds of those who do manage to enter school fail to complete three years of schooling. While it will take a massive effort to change this situation, as an interim measure, ICTs can be employed in formal and informal settings to deliver essential knowledge and information. The National Open School in India, using print, audio, local tutors, and ICT-based assessment and testing system on-call, provides postprimary education to remote villages throughout India. About 400,000 children have access to education up to grade-12 equivalence, and lessons prepared by teams of highly qualified teachers are made available to students free or at very low cost.

Taking Education to Girls

Gender disparity in educational access is a major challenge in many communities because of family and social circumstances. Inequalities between women and men extend from literacy classes to access to formal schooling and prospects for completing school. Social, cultural, religious, and economic factors all combine to create barriers and place girls and women at a serious disadvantage. While such barriers will take time to remove, ICTs provide one way to circumvent them. Learning and training will have to find their way to girls and women where they are located, rather than expecting them to come to places where teaching is conducted. The Allama Iqubal Open University of Pakistan approached the challenge of illiteracy among women in Pakistan through a unique combination of print, audio, radio, and mentors. Though all the technologies used were analog, the opportunity to digitize this effort and deliver it through local telelearning centers offers immense opportunities, in both qualitative and quantitative terms, to scale-up the effort.

Increasingly, ICTs are being recognized and used to bring education and training to those individuals who are challenged in one way or another. These tools include digital voice control software, audio to visual conversions for the hearing impaired, electronic text, and digital audio. The technologies, either stand-alone or as part of integrated systems, help to overcome barriers such as instruction based only on print and dependent on sight, audio dependent on hearing, and video requiring vision. The systems themselves have to be developed for individual use, so they require careful study of individual students' needs. Vincent describes a few such approaches taken by the developing countries Open University where print-based courses are adapted using ICT to enable challenged individuals to benefit from them.

Providing Education for Out-of-School Youth Education of out-of-school youth, especially beyond the basic level, can benefit from the application of ICTs. Vocational and trade skills, competency-based training, and alternate entry paths to higher education can be achieved through creation of knowledge products for a variety of situations, from self-learning to flexible learning environments. Multimedia commercial training products are becoming increasingly available for training in vocational skills. Governments can play an important role in enabling vocational training institutes, encouraging nongovernmental organizations (NGOs) engaged in supporting youth development, and prodding media outlets to use ICTs for youth training and personal development.

Creating Open and Virtual Learning Environments Smart schools, online education, and virtual universities are labels that have been attached to institutes applying a new set of strategies to deliver education using digital networks either synchronously or asynchronously. The technologies are used to deliver instruction, to manage the system's administrative services, and to provide support for learners. The last four decades have seen the emergence of colleges and universities dedicated to delivering tertiary-level education off-campus to learners, especially in those countries where the gap between the supply of and demand for tertiary-level education is huge and largely unmet. These universities apply open learning principles and distance education practices to deliver learning. They are generally universities with big student populations comprising mature and mostly part-time learners. Ten of the largest universities in the world are open universities, and all but one of them is located in developing countries. In total, they may have as many as 2 million students enrolled in their programs.

ICTs have always played an important role in managing and administering these universities, and older analog technologies such as radio and video also have been used to enrich the learning environment of the open universities. With the arrival of the newer digital technologies, ICTs also have begun to figure much more intensely in this role.

One of the most powerful reasons for considering using ICTs in an educational system is that they put learning in the hands of the user. They facilitate individualizing curriculum, permit learners to dictate the pace of learning, and widen sources of information. ICTs also promote active learning and allow for interaction between and among peers and mentors. Many would say as well that the quality and effectiveness of learning is enhanced many times through the use of ICTs. The technologies allow faculty to incorporate new information and update learning materials, and they enable immediate and rapid transfer of information pertaining to the administration of a course or program of study. Of these many educational objectives, the five below stand out as extremely important.

Learning to know, learning to do, learning to be, and learning to live together are all ideals that are achievable with in the framework of basic and postbasic education. These recommendations recognize that today's learners, young and old, will spend their lives in a century that is information-rich, knowledge–dependent, and global. They need the skills to cope with this dynamic period. The growth of online library systems, easy access to expert knowledge through the Web, the variety of sources of learning, and frequent change of careers and location of residence during a person's productive lifetime will necessitate learning new skills and refreshing old skills. The curriculum should reflect these concerns and will include:

— The ability to frame problems when facing unfamiliar situations. Tomorrow's problems may be similar to yesterday's once they are well understood. But these present themselves in new forms. Once a problem has been framed, it must be solved and, often, both framing and solving problems will require powerful information technologies. Framing and solving problems sometimes will be simpler, but they often are likely to be more difficult than before.

— The ability to communicate, including with people from other groups. Nations' ethnic composition is becoming more diverse, and increasing globalization has meant having frequent contact with people of other nations and cultures. All of this requires sensitivity to numerous cultures, and some common and shared values and insights, if political and social tensions are to be avoided and conflicts minimized.

— The ability to work in, form, and lead teams and coalitions, including involving people of other cultures. This vital skill is seldom taught comprehensively in schools, and, as global interdependence increases in importance, so, too, does collaboration.

— The ability to identify what needs to be learned, and then learn it efficiently. ICTs often will furnish the means for learning. Every educated person will need to spend a certain fraction of his or her life keeping up with changes in that technology.

In all these areas, ICTs are an extremely invaluable asset. The Web, more than any other tool we know of, has the power to make enormous amounts of information from their original source available at the click of a button. This information, in its multimedia form, provides teachers and learners with information to support and enrich curriculum in the modern classroom. Subscriptions to digital libraries, collaborative projects with peers outside of one's own classroom, and access to remote knowledge and expertise make lessons richer in content and, in the process, learning more exciting.

The time-driven, rigid organizational structures of our institutions of learning, our assumptions of learning, and our traditions of teaching, as well as the urban location of 65 teaching institutions, have combined to present barriers of one kind or another to learning for all but a small proportion of citizens. The new ICTs provide enormous flexibility of use unlike older technologies, which required learners to be assembled in a controlled environment at a specific time and location. Radio and television had to be tied rigidly to schedules developed centrally. On the other hand, the new technologies are available for use 'anytime, anywhere.' The emergence of virtual education is very much a reflection of this versatility: Learners can access their education or training at the workplace, home, library, or anywhere connection to a telephone and power supply is available.

Transformation in the Teaching/Learning Process

Learning technologies can affect education in systemic and structural ways. The challenge for educators is to bring about a balance among content learning, technology learning, and social experience. This balance depends on instructional strategies that accommodate individual learning styles and, at the same time, provide for effective assessment. Successful introduction of ICTs into the learning environment also includes support for interdisciplinary interaction with peers and instructors and among groups. This arrangement allows learners to interact with their institutions and their communities.

The newer technologies can change the relationship between teachers and learners to improve the learning process and learning experience. Traditional teaching and learning habits always have favored a certain passivity. Professors lectured and students listened and took notes; sometimes they asked questions, but they seldom contributed to knowledge. That was also true for the older technologies of print, radio, and television, despite the hype given them. Though active and independent learning were aspired to, they were hard to achieve, given the limitation of the technology. New ICTs make it possible for students to be active learners. Both teachers and students can control, manipulate, and contribute to information and knowledge generation. Using ICTs, students not only make choices about the pace and order of a presentation, but also may choose topics for explorations; take notes; answer questions; explore virtual landscapes; simulate experiments; enter, draw, or chart data; create and manipulate images; make their own PowerPoint presentations; and communicate with others.

ICTs have great capacity to facilitate the educational transaction between providers and users. For instance, ICTs can be used to:

— Keep students well informed about the courses that are available to them.

— Enhance teacher-learner contact, an essential part of a good educational environment, through e-mail, chat sessions, etc.

— Encourage active learning. Students do not learn much from memorizing facts and reproducing set answers; they derive greater benefits by being active in their learning.

— Facilitate peer support in learning. Sharing one's ideas and responding to the ideas of others improves thinking and increases understanding. Learning can improve if it is a team effort rather than a collection of solo performances.

— Provide immediate feedback and encouragement.

— Encourage paced learning through tools such as assignments, tutorials, broadcast programs, computers, conferencing, etc.

— Allow for effective mapping of learning pathways, which facilitate different styles of learning.

Professional Development of Teachers

Like all other professions, teachers need constant and continuous renewal to be effective, motivated, and up to date in their knowledge and skills. While this is not a mandatory requirement in many national jurisdictions, those that do have such requirements use and see ICTs as important vehicles to provide continuing professional development to teachers. The use of ICTs, especially in support of distance education activities, adds enormous value to the training. Where the infrastructure exists, and connectivity costs are subsidized, the opportunity to create virtual online learning communities of teachers within nations and across regions exists. Such learning communities enable and empower trainee and practicing teachers to share experience, curriculum, learning materials, lesson notes.

ICTs can be applied in at least three training contexts:

— basic training, upgrading and advancing pedagogical skills and content knowledge, and continuous professional development.

Resource sharing

Until the arrival of the computer, sharing knowledge, an important basis of education, was more wishful than real. With ICTs, sharing knowledge resources is enhanced many times over. Putting information on the Web makes it available immediately to anyone in the world with a suitable connection. Teachers can share lesson plans with their colleagues in their own jurisdictions and with those far removed from their jurisdictions. Students from all over the world can undertake joint projects, exchange findings, analyze data collectively, and draw reasoned conclusions. Knowledge about and of interest to minority groups, languages, and interests can enjoy the same opportunity to publish and share.

Lifelong learning is a necessity in a world that changes and renews itself so rapidly. Such dynamism makes demands on individuals to update themselves constantly in the context of their workplace, social life, and participation in healthy and vibrant democracies. Two broad categories of individuals use lifelong learning opportunities.

— To those who are underrepresented across a whole range of postbasic education and includes, among others, illiterate and neoliterate populations engaged in unskilled work; ethnic, marginalized, and minority groups; people with learning difficulties; and the physically challenged. These learners face such obstacles as lack of learning skills, confidence, money, counseling and advice, and personal support, and they require active intervention by the state, the business sector, and voluntary organizations.

— To those who have had the benefit of some form of postbasic education but are not equipped to deal effectively with the technology-driven environment in which they find themselves. This group includes out-of-school youth, employees in workplaces, individuals with basic training, professionals needing continuing education, and older adults seeking personal enrichment. These people are expected to know their needs, but they face challenges such as inadequate supply of learning opportunities, inflexibility of learning systems, lack of money, and inadequate supply of information. There is increasing evidence that ICTs are beginning to play an effective role in promoting lifelong learning. Supported by a greater bandwidth capacity, digital and interactive radio and television, and multimedia, pathways are extending the speed with which learning products can be delivered to learners over large catchment areas. However, to make this happen, some basic conditions need to be met, including regulatory frameworks, infrastructure, affordable cost structures, public access to multimedia facilities, skills training in ICT use and employer support, and institutional commitment of learning providers.

The rapid changes taking place in the workplace will require training to be delivered quickly. Such training needs to be highspeed, low-cost, and accessible to small and large groups. Traditional ways of delivering training are time-consuming, labor-intensive, socially disruptive, and expensive. Workers have to acquire new skills quickly and affordably. It becomes even more attractive if such training can be delivered at the trainees' workplace. Also, adult learners require flexibility, and they have families, work commitments, and social obligations around which they have to fit their training. This simply means that, ideally, training has to be accessible anywhere, anytime. Just-in-time-training is especially relevant in the context of business and industrial training where there is a continuous need to respond quickly to demands from the work environment.

Facilitating Nonformal Education

ICTs are being used to make information and knowledge

available in nonformal contexts. The demand for enrichment learning is on the rise, particularly in countries experiencing an increase in aging populations and in populations with more leisure time who want to use it in intellectual pursuits. These are learners for pleasure, and, for them, activities in a classroom are not the ideal solutions. ICTs offer a convenient solution, but only if the individual has the skills needed to use the appliances and navigate through the millions of Web pages and is able to pay for the cost of the digital connection. Besides structured learning for enrichment purposes, unstructured learning opportunities are increasingly available through zoos, museums, planetariums, research institutions, professional societies, interest groups, commercial companies, and national agencies, among others.

The knowledge to be gained can range from virtual tours of, for example, archeological sites to the epidemiology of HIV/AIDS. It is as possible to learn to cook exotic food as it is to design and make quilts. One can participate in a debate on the World Trade Organization organized by supporters or detractors or engage in a discussion with a Nobel laureate on rain forest exploitation. All of these learning opportunities inform citizens, enrich their lives, enable them to share indigenous knowledge, and empower them to participate in functioning democracies.

Even as recently as 10 years ago, the choice of technologies for delivering education was somewhat limited, partly because they were expensive, analog stand-alones with limited versatility, and they required skilled technicians to create and deliver the product. Radio and television are prime examples of the demand these technologies made on educational systems. Those that did not fall into this category, such as overhead projectors, slide projectors, etc., had limited reach. Today the picture has changed almost completely. Technology application in education no longer is limited by the versatility, convenience, cost, and potential of the technology but, rather, only by our imagination in the way technology can be applied. Through integration, convergence, miniaturization, and intelligence, technologies have become friendly. Digitization of many information and communication technologies has made it possible to design, develop, deliver, manage, and assess the learning and training process.

The new digital technologies are not single technologies; they are combinations of hardware and software, media, and delivery systems. They are evolving and converging rapidly, as seen in PCs, laptops, notebooks, and digital cameras that are both video and single-image; local area networking; the World Wide Web; CD-ROMs and DVDs; application software, such as word processing, spreadsheets, and simulations; e-mail; digital libraries; and computer-mediated conferencing, videoconferencing, and virtual reality. They also have a capacity to integrate with older analog technologies from print, and through audio and video, make it possible to retrieve information stored in older technologies and to develop synergies between the old and the new. There are excellent reviews of the older analog technologies, which still have tremendous value, especially in many developing countries and their educational systems.

Let us focus on newer technologies, which are mostly available to and used in developed countries for education, but hold tremendous promise globally in both

both rich and poor communities. They also differ in several important aspects from older technologies in their integration of multimedia, convergence of communication and information technologies, interactivity, flexibility of use, and connectivity. Understanding these differences will help us to appreciate why the use of ICT in education is expected to grow. ICTs for teaching and learning range from those that rely on ubiquitous low-cost technology, such as the stand-alone PC, to those deployed for specific purposes at higher cost, such as the electronic classroom. Decisions on the choice of technologies are subject to many considerations and constraints, ranging from constancy of power supply to availability of skilled technical and managerial support to maintaining the technological infrastructure. Assuming these are available, then questions of pedagogical strategies of the system, accessibility, scale, and cost will play a role in the choice. Some of the newer IC technologies available and used today are discussed below.

E-mail

Increasingly, e-mail is becoming the most widely used medium, ranging in function from exchange of gossip, to serious dialogue and collaborative research. It also has become an important supplement to classroom teaching. Bulletin board services extend the classroom beyond fixed timetables; listservs bring communities of learners together; and assignments and term papers are beginning to be channeled routinely through e-mail. On-campus education is being enriched by e-mail facilities, and off-campus education is made more personal and interactive. In economically developed countries, e-mail is almost as common as the telephone. In many cases, connections are free of charge, appliances are provided at low or no cost, and training is available for neophyte users. In poor economies, e-mail has yet to make its presence felt throughout society, but is increasingly available at community service centers such as libraries, telelearning centers, and "cyber cafes."

PowerPoint and similar programs are already commonplace among academics and other professionals. While a simple slide presentation requires little skill to develop, the increasing sophistication level of such a presentation requires higher-level training.

World Wide Web

Many on-campus instructors are beginning to use the Web to make their lecture notes available to students at any time. The Web also has the advantage of providing access to primary sources of information in most media (print, graphics, photographs, audio, and video) through streaming. This technology requires good organizational and pedagogical skills to profit from its enormous potential, and faculty training in its use will be essential. Bates considers the Web to be a low-cost technology for several reasons: the existence of simple computer languages such as HTML and intermediary course authoring systems such as the WebCT and Blackboard; it uses the Internet as a transport vehicle that involves no direct charge for independent packets of information, and pricing is by volume and not by time or distance; the Web's ability to combine media, thereby increasing its range of applications; access to high-quality learning resources inexpensively; it allows asynchronous interpersonal communication through e-mail, bulletin 69 boards, and discussion forums; and it enables cross-cultural, international, collaborative learning.

Multimedia, CD-ROM, DVD

Multimedia, CD-ROMs, and DVDs are very exciting learning tools. Their development costs can be very high, especially those at the very high end that can carry large quantities of data in a variety of formats, such as audio and video clips, Internet connections to other databases, large amounts of information, and built-in simulation and other enrichments. Putting all these together in user-friendly packages will require teams of experts, from media producers to content experts. The reproduction cost of CD-ROMs can be reduced considerably if large numbers are "burned." Consequently, this medium is a consideration only when enrollments are large enough to justify the development expense. However, there is a strong case for developing the medium when the course can be used by a consortium of institutions working together.

Under the right conditions and used properly, the technologies can be highly effective as both teaching and learning tools. The challenge for institutions is to develop the knowledge and skills to exploit the technologies' full potential. At the heart of all learning that uses ICTs are materials specially designed to exploit the full potential of the available technologies. These materials normally include content in the form of texts, special "books of readings," specially developed study or learner's guides, assignments and assessments pads, and instructor's or tutor's guides. These resources, along with appropriate learner support systems, complete the educational or training environment. There are two ways by which institutions acquire these learning and teaching resources: they design and develop them either by themselves or in partnership with like-minded collaborators, or they purchase, lease, or acquire—through other arrangements—materials already developed and adapt them for their unique needs.

Developing interactive multimedia learning materials is an exceedingly interesting challenge. They can be constructed from a combination of media, sometimes quite modest in cost and sophistication, such as a combination of computer-aided instruction (CAI) and print, and at other times very expensive and elaborate, using a combination of DVD, CD-ROM, hypermedia, and virtual reality. Such is the case with interactive video, where the assembled team includes instructional designers who speak of authoring, pedagogics and remediation; graphic artists who talk of drop shadows, GUI's and animated sprites; video producers who think in terms of wipes, fades, pictures, plots, scenes and storylines; and computer specialists who deal in bits and bytes, images and data, icons, picons, microns and programming language all their own.

For well over three decades now, and long before the arrival of the newer technologies, dedicated distance teaching institutions such as the open universities of the UK, Canada, India, Thailand, Turkey, Israel, South Africa, and other countries have been developing courses using a variety of media. The experience gained through these institutions is just as relevant in today's technology-rich environment, where digitization allows for totally seamless integration, as it was then in an analog world. Unlike face-to-face teaching, the design and development of interactive multimedia materials involves the knowledge, skills, and expertise of a number of individuals. Therefore, assembling a team to undertake the task is almost a prerequisite if a high-quality product is the ultimate objective.

The size of the team, and the skills of the individuals who make up the team, will depend on the sophistication of the product to be developed. It is possible, though not advisable—as is often the case in many small operations—for one person (normally the content expert) to create the learning materials. At a minimum, the course team should have a content expert and an instructional designer. In addition to content experts and instructional designers, complex course team composition may involve audio and video producers, editors, ICT specialists, publishers. The team approach will require a totally different work culture from what is normally associated with academe.

Digitization of knowledge products opens up unprecedented opportunities for their portability. CD-ROMS, DVDs, and other multimedia have the capacity to carry entire courses on a single disc. Furthermore, granulation of knowledge allows for greater manipulation of the content to suit particular needs and clients. There are also economies to be gained. However, acquiring knowledge products from other sources for local use requires careful consideration of many issues and factors, besides intellectual property rights and 72 economic concerns; sometimes it is cheaper to produce courses in house than to purchase and adapt them.

4

Globalisation and Education

Education systems must help to build higher-order cognitive abilities, strengthen processes of inquiry, enable collaborative problem solving, and prepare people to compete in local and global markets and become productive members of society. Providing citizens with quality education is becoming ever more important with globalization and the increasingly dominant role information, knowledge, and digital technologies play in all economies. A new gap is arising between those who have access to and can use modern information and communication technology (ICT) systems and those who lack the access and ability to participate actively in the Information Age. No single solution exists to address the immense challenges of providing quality education and bridging the ICT gap.

One possibility is to develop and apply new approaches and strategies for teaching and learning that integrate computers, Internet-enabled collaborative learning, and related educational technologies with routine teaching and learning. When used effectively and integrated into education, computers and Internet technologies can improve teaching and learning, strengthen teacher professional development, support broad educational reform, enhance school-community partnerships, and improve school management. The demand to realize these educational objectives by integrating computer and Internet technologies into education forces education planners, principals, teachers, and technology specialists to make many decisions about the technical, training, financial, pedagogical, and infrastructure requirements of school computerization programs.

Some of the more challenging questions planners and educators must answer have to do with infrastructure issues. In this chapter, infrastructure includes what types of computer hardware to use, where and how computers should be distributed and networked in schools, if and how school computers can and should be connected to the Internet, and the software choices schools need to make. This chapter also touches on policies that can help to develop enabling environments to support school computerization and connectivity programs. There is no single best computer configuration or single infrastructure solution to suit all situations. Rather, there are only optimum solutions for each school. Arriving at these optimum solutions is not simply a technical process but requires a careful consideration of educational goals and an understanding of the different costs and benefits, both economic and educational, of different technology options.

School Context

Since infrastructural questions are dominated by a complex mix of technical factors, requirements, and options, decisions about infrastructure often are divorced from educational concerns and driven by technical matters and technology experts. In reality, infrastructure questions and decisions are coupled with educational needs, opportunities, and outcomes. Therefore, to achieve optimum educational results, each school or school system should base infrastructure decisions on an assessment of a mix of technical factors and educational needs and objectives.

The results of such an assessment then must be compared to the costs and benefits of a variety of computer system configurations and infrastructure options. When carrying out an educational/ infrastructure assessment, the following questions may need to be considered:

— *Educational goals:* Different computer configurations have direct relationships to how computers and the Internet can and will be used by teachers and students to enhance education.

— *Professional development:* Enhancing teacher professional development by training teachers both to use computer and Internet technologies and to integrate these technologies into education, along with improving subject matter competence and strengthening pedagogical skills, are often important objectives of school computer programs. Ensuring that such objectives are achieved often requires that teachers be provided with special access to computer and Internet technologies and a complex mix of initial and ongoing training and support. If online professional development is planned, suitable Internet connectivity and time to engage in online learning will be required.

— *Student-to-computer ratio:* Most schools calculate this ratio by simply dividing the number of students in the school by the number of computers available to students. This simple calculation may not present an accurate picture of students' productive access to computers, however. In secondary schools, the issue is viewed more appropriately in terms of how much computer and Internet access, frequency, and duration students in different disciplines have.

— *Other physical conditions:* One of the major questions about school computer systems focuses on whether to install computers in classrooms or computer labs. If classrooms are small and crowded and without lockable doors, it may be more appropriate to use labs. Creating optimum lighting conditions, especially where electrical light may be difficult to manage, often can be achieved most easily by modifying computer labs for skylights rather than trying to adjust the lighting in every room in a school. Often, as described below, the simplest way to connect computers to the Internet is through telephone lines and a dial-up connection to an Internet service provider (ISP). However without existing phone lines, it can prove difficult and expensive to provide wiring for telephone connections in more than just one or two computer labs.

— *Physical security:* Providing sufficient security in the classroom and at the school to prevent theft of equipment, software, and supplies can be expensive and it is often only possible for one or two rooms in a school. When security plans are made, it is important to achieve a balance between protecting equipment from theft and allowing easy access to computers as often as possible. Fears of being blamed for damage to or loss of equipment can cause principals and teachers to make it very difficult for students to use computers, or for community members to benefit from investments in technology through after-school use.

— *Students per classroom:* Schools with large numbers of students per classroom are likely to have limited space for permanently installed computers. Under such conditions, it may be best to install computers in one or more lab facilities where students can use the equipment. For smaller children, it is possible to have two to four students per computer. However, it is difficult and restrictive to have more than two older students per computer. To allow multiple students per computer requires sufficient space between computers with enough room left over to allow teachers to move among students to review work and offer support and feedback.

— *School's electrical system:* Computers operate better and last longer when the electricity that powers them is continuous and of consistent voltage. Many schools, especially older ones, have an insufficient supply of electricity to withstand the additional demand made by the computers.

Further, electrical cables may not be the correct gauge to withstand the additional load caused by computers being connected to the school's electrical system. Or the electrical cables may be composed of aluminum, which oxidizes over time and can become a fire hazard. Lack of electricity or poor wiring may require the school to refurbish the existing electrical system or add a whole new electrical supply system. This is one reason why many schools decide to install computers in labs, which reduces the amount of electrical wiring needed. Also, computers, especially those connected to a local area network (LAN), require a grounded electrical system to operate smoothly and trouble-free. Again, this is less costly if done to one or two computer labs or rooms, rather than to the entire school.

The quality of electricity coming to a school also may be inconsistent and fluctuate between low and high voltages. These conditions can disrupt students' use of computers and result in premature and sudden failure of expensive computer equipment. These problems are often dealt with by installing line stabilizers to make the voltage constant and uninterruptible power supplies to provide a short-term (10 to 20 minutes) supply of electricity to the computer to allow work to be saved and equipment to be turned off safely when the electrical supply fails. Adding this equipment to a school computerization plan can increase costs significantly. When electricity is not available, it may be possible to install solar-powered systems for the computer equipment. Solar equipment can be very expensive and is often best used with laptop computers, since they use less power and can use direct current (DC) electricity directly. Also, since laptops come with their own batteries, less money may need to be spent on a battery backup system for the solar panels.

— *Special-needs or disabled students:* Learning-disabled students may need special keyboards with large keys and audio and tactile feedback to engage the technology effectively. Computer technologies have had some of their greatest impact in educating special-needs students. However, ignoring their special mobility and technological needs at the start of the planning and design process will guarantee that these benefits will be unrealized.

— *Temperature and air quality:* Modern computers and cathode ray tube monitors generate a great deal of heat. The lack of sufficient ventilation, especially in humid climates, can result in a very uncomfortable working environment for students and, occasionally, can even cause computers to overheat and malfunction. However, opening windows to improve air circulation can result in a damaging level of dust entering the computer room and increased risk of equipment theft. The combination of heat and dust often forces school computer programs to install expensive air conditioning units. Before committing to the purchase of air conditioning systems, programs should consult with architects, often as volunteers, about alternative strategies suitable for local environments to keep computer labs comfortable and free of excessive dust.

— *Connecting computers together:* Connecting computers together in a local area network (LAN), can have significant educational benefits. At the same time, creating a LAN has financial and infrastructure effects that need to be weighed carefully against possible educational gains. LANs, if carefully planned, can be installed after the initial computer system is put in place if funding prohibits installation at the start. However, careful planning will be needed to avoid any duplication of effort and wasted investment.

— *Internet connectivity:* The sustainability of any scheme to introduce computers into the educational process depends on careful attention to technical support and to equipment maintenance and renewal.

— *Financial resources:* Technology budgets for initial installation of systems and ongoing support likely will be a decisive factor when deciding which configuration is best for a school or school system. As a result, budgets for ongoing equipment support, supply, repair, and replacement often are neglected or insufficient. Also, funds to purchase and install equipment and provide initial teacher training may come from national or state budgets. In contrast, local government and school budgets often will have to cover the purchase of consumables, pay for connectivity, and fund technical support and maintenance to keep the systems running.

Without additional funds, these ongoing responsibilities and recurrent expenses often are not met. It may be necessary, therefore, for schools to devise special fund-raising schemes such as opening up the computer system to fee-based use during nonschool hours, reaching out to parent-teacher associations (PTAs), and soliciting the local business community for funding.

In addition, where families have sufficient disposable income, some schools have charged an annual computer use fee to cover the cost of consumables and equipment maintenance. No matter what the solution, schools should develop and implement strategies immediately to guarantee sustainability of their computer systems.

— *Educator technology skills:* Only knowing how to use the technology will not enable teachers to use computer and Internet technologies to enhance learning significantly. Initial and ongoing teacher professional development focusing on using computers and effective pedagogy usually is required to enable schools to gain the greatest educational benefit from their investments in computers. The configuration of computer facilities plays a major role in providing effective learning opportunities and professional development for teachers.

— *School routine:* Using computer labs and/or placing computers in classrooms permit teachers to organize students into a variety of learning activities, some using computers and others not; and make it easier to individualize instruction and strategically integrate computer and Internet technologies into project-based learning.

Achieving the multiple benefits of classroom-based computers demands significant financial investments to:

— purchase sufficient hardware and software so that all classes have equal access to computers;

— refurbish all classrooms so that there is sufficient room for the computers and a suitable electrical supply, security, networkability, and connectivity;

— provide each teacher with a high degree of computer technical and pedagogical skills since education technology specialists will not be available to help as they would in a computer lab; and

— supply ongoing technical and educational support.

Unfortunately, not all schools can afford enough computers to enable effective student access and use. As a result, some schools may decide to install only one or two computers per classroom, which likely will have little or no impact on learning. Experience also shows that when there is only a single computer in a classroom, it often becomes the "teacher's" computer and is rarely used by students.

Considerations for installing computers in classrooms include:

— *Teachers' skills:* Computers in classrooms usually require teachers to have a high degree of technical skill and the capacity to integrate computer use into their teaching.

— *Space and student numbers:* Placing clusters of computers in a classroom to enable effective student use requires enough space for both the computer systems and groups of two to three students to sit comfortably in front of the computers, circulation area for teachers and nontraditional student seating arrangements.

— *Quality and availability of electricity:* Computers demand a quality electrical supply. Remodeling classrooms to meet the electrical needs of computers is usually very expensive, especially if it needs to be done in many classrooms.

— *Security:* Maintaining sufficient security to prevent theft of equipment, software, and supplies, while also enabling open access to the classrooms to a variety of users, is usually impossible.

Distributing computers throughout the classrooms in a school makes it more difficult, and more expensive, to provide effective maintenance and support services dealt with at the very start of devising a school computer plan. One of the most difficult challenges, however, is balancing educational objectives with technical limitations and hard financial realities. Ultimately, the goal of assessing objectives, needs, conditions, and options is to determine the optimum configuration for integrating computers into education at a specific school. There are many ways to describe different infrastructure needs and computer system configuration options and strategies.

Physical Configuration Options

Computers can be distributed in schools in three basic ways to meet educational goals. They can be provided to individual classrooms; installed in central computer labs, libraries, and teachers' planning rooms; or moved from room to room on mobile carts. Each of these options, and combinations of them, has associated benefits and costs that need to be considered carefully to select the options that best meet a school's needs. Some educational technology specialists argue that proximity and easy access to computers achieved by placing them in classrooms are crucial in achieving high rates of student and teacher use and, thus, educational benefits. Similarly, some people think installing computers in central computer rooms or labs is "old fashioned" and inhibits effective educational use. These are overly simplistic perspectives because the distribution of computers is only one factor in determining how teachers and students use them, and the Internet, to enhance teaching and learning.

One of the greatest potential benefits of distributing computers to individual classrooms is to provide teachers and students with easier access to these educational tools. More specifically, having computers in classrooms can:

— make it easier for teachers to integrate computer and Internet use into routine educational programs—but this cannot be guaranteed;

— allow for spontaneous use of these tools during instructional activities;

— *Internet access:* Providing even limited Internet access in each classroom via intermittent use of a single dial-up phone connection can be expensive, and highspeed access can become prohibitive.

— *Connecting computers within the classroom and the school:* Most schools require extensive remodeling to enable computers in classrooms and schools to be connected to form cabled networks. Also, creating classroom networks can require significant investments in additional hardware (servers, hubs, routers, etc.).

School-based Computer Systems

Installing computers in classrooms can make it more difficult to provide community access to these costly resources. This difficulty is exacerbated if the number of computers per classroom is relatively low, since no single room may have a sufficient number of computers to meet community use and training needs. As a result, schools with classroom-based computers may not be able to generate enough revenue to cover the costs of consumables, maintenance, and replacement of systems through community access to their computers. With sufficient funding, and under the right conditions, with highly skilled teachers, classroom-based computers can have a significant impact on the quality of teaching and learning.

Classroom-based computer installations with low student-to-computer ratios also can provide unparalleled student access to computer use and enable teachers to integrate the use of computers and the Internet in ways that cannot be achieved by any other configuration. However, for most schools, especially those in developing countries and poor communities, it isn't possible to install computers routinely in classrooms. Under these more common conditions, alternative strategies must be considered.

Computer Rooms or Labs

Establishing one or more computer rooms or labs is a popular way to provide equitable access to computers for the greatest number of users at the lowest possible cost. Computer labs enable schools to concentrate expensive resources in a common space that can be used for student educational activities, teacher professional development events, and community groups. When using computer labs, it is important to arrange computers along the walls of the room rather than in rows facing the front of the room, so teachers can view all the students' work from a common point and move quickly and easily from student to student, providing feedback, support, and guidance. This arrangement also can make it easier and less costly to provide electricity and network access for the computers. Some of the benefits and challenges of using computer labs are discussed below.

Benefits

— Establishing computers in a lab or dedicated room only requires schools to install quality electricity, network cabling and servers, Internet access, effective security, climate control systems, good lighting, and specialized furniture in one or two rooms in a school rather than in many different rooms.

— If designed effectively, a dedicated room ensures sufficient space to allow students to work in groups and move about to see each other's work, while also allowing teachers to move from group to group to provide input and guidance.

— Computer labs can be maintained by one or two staff members who also can provide technical and pedagogical support to teachers.

— Equipment and software can cost less for computer labs used by all classes than for classroom-based systems.

— Computer labs can optimize return on technology investments if their use is scheduled effectively.

— It can be easier and less costly to provide access to the Internet via computer labs than with classroom systems since many computers can use a common connection to the Internet.

— Computer labs can make it easier to encourage collaborative interdisciplinary projects among groups of teachers and students.

— Computer labs make it easier to provide community access to computer systems for public relations, and to generate revenue to cover the costs of consumables, Internet connectivity, and replacement of old equipment.

Challenges

— Computer labs can become oversubscribed quickly, and competition for use may make it difficult for teachers 82 to engage their students in longer-term projects and activities.

— Scheduling conflicts can frustrate teachers and inhibit their use of computer labs.

— Once the novelty of using computers wears off, encouraging teachers to move their students to the lab may become more difficult.

— Spontaneous need to use computers for research, reference, word processing, etc., can be difficult or impossible to accommodate.

— In some schools, principals or lab coordinators may implement policies designed to keep the computers safe at the expense of using them.

Schools can overcome many of the challenges of using school computer labs by devising and implementing effective policies governing the use of the labs. A computer lab coordinator is a critical asset and can continue to promote use of the lab and help teachers deal with scheduling conflicts. Labs also can include one or two open- or free-access computers that can be used by students and teachers without scheduling. Computers-on-Wheels (COWs)

Computers-on-Wheels (or COWs) systems are essentially rolling carts that hold one or more computers (often 10 to 20), usually laptops, often with a printer, and with the possibility to connect the cart to the school LAN via a single classroom network connection. COWs can be brought into a classroom, often by an educational technology specialist, when the teacher wants to use computers for a specific activity. Some of the benefits and challenges of using COWs are discussed below.

— COWs make it possible to provide teachers access to computers in their classroom without having to remodel the room significantly, provide special furniture, or reserve space for dedicated computers.

— Working in small groups at their desks enables all students to have access to computers even in crowded classrooms.

— Using battery-powered laptops makes it possible to avoid providing special electrical power or installing additional power outlets.

— Using infrared printing and wireless networking cards enables the students to print their work and connect to each other and the school network for e-mail, electronic communication, and, possibly, Internet access without cables.

— COWs allow schools to optimize the use of expensive equipment by enabling teachers to request a cart of computers.

— COWs may be more affordable than remodeling classrooms, building special computer labs, providing special electrical supplies, installing cabling to network all the computers, and buying special furniture.

— Since software only needs to be purchased for the computers on the carts, and not for dozens of computers in each classroom, the cost of software can be much less with COWs than with classroom-based installations.

— COWs can be stored in secure rooms when not in use.

— COWs can provide access to computers in situations where students have classes in different rooms.

— COWs can be customized to include expensive specialized equipment that normally would not be part of a classroom system.

— COWs often are brought to classrooms by an educational technology specialist who can help teachers to make effective use of the computers in teaching and provide immediate technical support.

— COWs can be used in teacher professional development programs.

— COWs can be used to support school-community computer programs because they can be brought to the room in the school used by community members.

For schools with few extra rooms for labs and no space or funds to build them, COWs offer a cost-effective way to provide teachers and students with access to computers and Internet connectivity. If COWs are used, effort should be made to promote the use of the COWs and to help teachers move beyond simple uses of computers in education. Without added educational inputs, COW systems can fall into disuse and rarely find their way into the classroom. Computers in Libraries and Teachers' Rooms When funding and staff resources are scarce, schools can optimize investments in computers and Internet access by installing a few computers in public spaces, such as the library or teachers' room. Giving teachers private access to computers and the Internet can encourage them to learn to use ·these technologies and integrate them into their daily routines.

Wherever possible, the greatest educational returns on technology investments can result by using combinations of the above configuration options. For schools with sufficient room, suitable infrastructure, and adequate funds and technical resources, distributing some computers to classrooms either as stationary systems or via COWs can be an effective means of easy and spontaneous access. Computer labs then can be used for whole class access and interdisciplinary use. Library computers can be used to focus on research activities, while special classrooms can be outfitted with computers, especially for special-needs students, creating benefits that are difficult to achieve from computer labs. The combination of these different options with one or more computer labs can create an ideal solution to providing students and teachers with access to these rich and powerful educational tools.

Networking Technology Options

Connecting computers together to form a network, and connecting school, lab, and classroom networks to the Internet can multiply the educational value and impact of computers in schools. There are a variety of options for creating classroom, lab, and school computer LANs.

As with all networked computers, users can share files and resources located on computers in the network.

With peer-to-peer networking, however, there is no file server or central computer to manage network activity. One or more of the computers in a peer-to-peer network can provide centralized services such as printing and access to the Internet. Most desktop operating systems come with software to enable peer-to-peer networking once the computers are connected by some cable or wireless networking infrastructure.

Peer-to-peer networking is good for small networks where a centralized file server is not needed and network security is not a major issue. This type of networking is less expensive to set up since the only additional expense is in the cables and networking hardware (one or two hubs). Most common computer operating systems come with software to establish a peer-to-peer network, so it may not be necessary to purchase, install, and configure special network operating system software such as Windows NT, Novell Netware, or Linux.

As a computer network grows in size and complexity, it may be necessary to shift to a client/server style of network using more advanced network operating software. One of the advantages of client/server networks is that they are scalable: more clients and servers can be added to the system without changing the network significantly. These centralized networks are easier to manage, administer, and secure than peer-to-peer networks. These benefits come with some disadvantages, however. Because of the need to have a central "dedicated" server, initial costs are higher. Also, they are more complex to set up and maintain than stand-alone computers and peer-to-peer networks, often requiring schools to hire a technician to oversee the network. Also, if the server fails, all network functions fail.

A thin-client/server network is similar to a traditional client/server network except that the client is not a freestanding computer capable of operating on its own. In contrast, thin clients are desktop appliances or network devices that link the keyboard, monitor, and mouse to a server where all applications and data are stored, maintained, and processed. The server, often called an application server, is built to provide all networking services and computer calculations.

Since all network and computer services are centralized, all maintenance and upgrading is done at the server; there is no need to service the clients. Proponents of thin-client/server networks emphasize that even though initial purchase costs are usually higher than with traditional PC/server networks, lifetime costs or total cost of ownership can be significantly less. A low cost of ownership in this case is achieved primarily through a reduced cost of centralized management, which can be from centralized remote sites, and from less costly software and applications upgrades.

Thin-client/server networks are also easier to install than traditional client/server networks. In addition, since the client appliances cannot function without the server, there is little risk of theft. Thin-client systems are very efficient at providing access to the Internet, and, because the client appliances have few moving parts and limited functions, thin-client/server networks are more reliable and stable than traditional network systems. A major disadvantage of some thin-client/server networks is that little educational software is written to run on thin-85 client servers running a version of UNIX. Most of these servers come with special emulation software, but this is usually an incomplete solution: software often runs slower and some applications fail to function.

Since many thin-client/ server networks are based on a type of UNIX operating system, skills with UNIX are needed to set up and administer. However, if schools have no staff with these skills, but do have access to the Internet, it is possible to have a technician at some remote site administer and maintain the network. This enables a school district to have one highly skilled technician manage thin- client/server networks in several schools, thus reducing management costs further. Even though thin-client/server network systems are relatively uncommon in K-12 educational environments, they are a viable alternative to traditional client/server network systems. A careful assessment of total cost of ownership and the availability of technical skills at a school or school system can help planners decide if the thin-client/ server network is best for their needs.

There are essentially three ways to connect computers to form LANs: cables, wireless, and power line systems.

Cabled LANs

Installing cabling in older buildings or in schools with thick walls built of brick and cement can be expensive, difficult, and time-consuming. To provide a sufficient number of individual connections for each computer, and to allow for flexible arrangement of computers in a room, many ports and cables must be installed. Each cable connected to a computer must be connected as well to a network hub, an electronic device that controls the flow of network traffic between individual computers and the system's server, usually in clusters of 20 to 30 cables. Several hubs can be connected together to allow larger numbers of computers to be networked together. Hubs usually are housed in shielded and locked network closets to protect the hubs and prevent people from accidentally rearranging the network cables.

Cabled networks provide reliable, highspeed—up to 100 Mb per second—transmission of network traffic. Because cable systems are more common than the other two options, it is usually possible to find firms and technicians with the skills needed to install quality cable LAN systems.

Wireless LANs

An increasingly popular alternative to cabled LANs is wireless networks. This type of system does not require cables to connect computers to each other and to the server and shared peripherals. Instead, wireless network adapters (receivers) are installed in all computers that will be part of the network (either as an internal network card or as a device that plugs into the computer's universal serial bus [USB] port). One or more wireless network hubs/transmitters are connected to the server, usually by a cable (several wireless network hubs can be connected to each other in a daisy chain). Network traffic is then transmitted by the hub to each computer and to and from the server. Wireless LANs have many advantages:

— They can be installed and configured in a very short time, since limited or no construction is needed.

— They allow for a high degree of flexibility. Computers, especially laptops, can be moved around a room or building, within the range of the network signal, without losing their connection to the LAN.

— They can be less costly to install and use than conventional cabled systems.

— They allow schools to create customized LAN systems covering single rooms or whole sections of the school. They also can be mixed with cabled systems to create greater flexibility.

Wireless LANs are not a perfect solution for all environments. The speed of network traffic depends on how many computers are using the hub's bandwidth simultaneously. Distance from the hub and thickness and character of walls between the transmitter and receiver can affect the speed and quality of the network signal significantly. Because of the benefits of wireless LANs and their growing popularity, the technology is improving rapidly, and new standards with higher transmission rates are emerging.

Over the next few years, the speed and range of transmission will increase, and reliability and security will improve. Wireless LANs will become an increasingly desirable LAN solution for school computer systems.

Power Line LANs

Another alternative to installing special network cables that recently has become a reliable technology for some situations is to use the existing power lines in the school to carry the network traffic. Power line networking (PLN) currently is capable of providing reliable network communication speeds between 250Kbps and 500Kbps for six to 20 network access points. Higher-speed systems, ranging from two to 12 Mbps, are also available. Equipment costs are higher than conventional and wireless networking technologies, but these are expected to fall as technical improvements are made and larger-scale systems become available. In some situations, the costs of using PLN can be less than installing cable or wireless systems.

Internet Access Options

By accessing the Internet, computers can become powerful communication devices with many educational applications. A variety of options and technologies should be considered when deciding whether and how to access the Internet. Simulated Internet. If direct connection to the Internet is not possible, for economic or technical reasons, students and teachers can still gain simulated access to a selection of Internet resources by copying valuable Websites to CD-ROMs. Then they can use the CDs to access these sites, thus simulating the Internet. For example, the Rio de Janeiro municipal school system provides schools that cannot access the Internet directly with a CD containing a selection of more than 100 Portuguese-language educational Websites.

The CDs, which are updated periodically, use the same browsers that are used with the Internet, so that when Internet access becomes available, teachers and students will have no difficulty using this technology. The "Internet" CDs also can make it easier for teachers to prepare structured educational activities using Websites since they can preview the resources quickly before the class session. In addition, this approach can focus student inquiry because students can explore the CD's resources but cannot surf freely beyond the scope of the activity or become distracted by noneducational Websites. Also, since these Internet resources are stored locally, no time is spent waiting for Websites to load. Even if Internet access is available, a CD with copied Websites can make it easier for students to access Internet resources rather than relying on a slow, congested connection.

Dial-up connection: The simplest and lowest-cost connection to the Internet is through dial-up access using a single standard phone line. A dial-up connection can provide Internet access to a single computer (for example, in a lab, classroom, teachers' room, or library) or, by using software on a server, networked computers can share this single connection. However, with a shared connection, access can become very slow, since the total available bandwidth (the total amount of data that can be moved through the network per unit of time) is divided among all the computers sharing the same Internet connection. If two or three phone lines are available, these lines can be combined using an analog router to enable multiple phone line access to an ISP, thus increasing available bandwidth.

Dedicated connection and other connectivity options: Schools can get faster and more reliable Internet access by using permanent 'dedicated' high-speed connections where they are available and affordable. A variety of dedicated high-bandwidth options may be available to schools, including integrated services digital network (ISDN), digital subscriber line (DSL), terrestrial wireless, digital cable, radio modem, and satellite access. Several new technologies offer the potential for developing countries to leapfrog earlier generations of equipment to provide connectivity. Terrestrial wireless and satellite technologies offer many advantages because they do not require installation of wireline networks. Satellite facilities also can be installed where communication is needed, even in remote and isolated areas, rather than waiting for terrestrial networks to be extended from the cities.

Terrestrial wireless

Cellular telephony has become the first and only telephone service for many people in developing countries, where it may be available much sooner than fixed-line service. However, cellular access is often quite costly, and bandwidth is limited. It is likely to be more practical for short bursts of use for e-mail communication than for surfing the Web.

Wireless local loop

Wireless local loop systems can be used to extend local telephone services to rural schools without laying cable or stringing copper wire. Thus, instead of a 87 fixed-line connection, schools would have a wireless link to the telecommunications network. Wireless local loop costs have decreased, making it competitive with copper. Wireless systems enable faster extension to new users than extending wire or cable; they also have a lower ratio of fixed to incremental costs than copper, making it easy to add more customers and serve transient populations. Wireless is also less vulnerable than copper wire or cable to accidental damage or vandalism.

Point-to-point wireless systems

If the telephone company does not provide wireless local loop, schools may be able to install or lease their own wireless links to the Internet. Point-to-point fixed wireless, such as microwave systems, can provide high-speed Internet access by connecting to an ISP's point of presence (POP). These fixed wireless links may be the least expensive means of getting high-speed Internet access if wireline services are not available.

Cordless

Short-range cordless extensions can provide the link from wireless outstations to subscriber premises; the DECT (digital European cordless telephone) technology standard also can allow the base station to act as a wireless private branch exchange (PBX) and reduce costs further.

Third-generation mobile networks are beginning to be introduced in some industrialized countries, and eventually may be made widely available in developing regions. They offer greatly increased bandwidth over existing mobile networks, with the possibility of Internet access to handheld devices such as portable phones, personal digital assistants, and small personal computers. However, the capital cost of upgrading existing networks is very high, and the price of access for Internet applications may be greater than for other options.

Satellite technologies

Very small aperture terminals (VSATS): Small satellite earth stations operating with geosynchronous satellites can be used for interactive voice and data as well as for broadcast reception. For example, banks in remote areas of Brazil are linked via VSATs, and the National Stock

Exchange in India links brokers with rooftop VSATs. VSATs for television reception (known as TVRO—television receive only) deliver broadcasting signals to viewers in many developing regions, particularly in Asia and Latin America. Internet via satellite: Internet gateways can be accessed via geostationary satellites.

High-speed downlink: A system designed by Hughes, known as DirecPC, uses a satellite to deliver high-bandwidth Internet content downstream to a VSAT from an ISP. Upstream connectivity is provided over existing phone lines. This approach is designed for rural areas with telephone service, but where bandwidth is very limited. Some rural schools in the United States are using DirecPC for Internet access.

Interactive access via VSAT: Several companies offer fully interactive Internet access via satellite; examples include Gilat, Hughes Gateway, and Tachyon. Systems typically are designed for small-business or home office use, but could be a solution for schools with no other communication options. For example, schools in Alaska and the Canadian Arctic access the Internet via satellite. The price of Internet access is likely to decline as new protocols are developed to make more efficient use of bandwidth and, thus, lower transmission costs for users.

Data broadcasting by satellite: Geosynchronous satellites designed for interactive voice and data can be used for data broadcasting as well. For example, the WorldSpace satellite system delivers digital audio directly to small radios. While one market for these products is people who can afford to subscribe to digital music channels, the systems also can be used to transmit educational programs in a variety of languages for individual reception or community redistribution. It can also be used to deliver Internet content; schools or telecenters can identify which Websites they want to view regularly, and WorldSpace broadcasts the data for reception via an addressable modem attached to the radio. WorldSpace has donated equipment and satellite time for pilot projects at schools and telecenters in Africa.

Global mobile personal communications systems: Using low earth-orbiting satellites, these systems provide voice and low-speed (typically 2400 to 9600 bps) data virtually anywhere, using handheld transceivers. However, the price per minute for these services is typically much higher than national terrestrial services, and the first generation of low earth-orbiting satellites (from Iridium and Globalstar) has very limited bandwidth.

Bandwidth on demand: Future satellite systems are being planned to provide bandwidth on demand. Constellations of low earth-orbiting satellites such as Teledesic and new generations of geosynchronous satellites such as Loral's Cyberstar and Hughes's Spaceway will be designed to offer bandwidth on demand for Internet access, videoconferencing, and distance education.

Wireline Technologies: Innovations in wireline technology make it possible to provide high-speed Internet access over telephone lines, rather than having to upgrade existing copper networks. These technologies may be used in urban areas where basic telephone service is available.

Integrated services digital network (ISDN): Regular twisted-pair copper telephone lines can carry two 64 kbps channels plus one 16 kbps signaling channel. One channel can be used for voice and one for fax or Internet access, or two can be combined for videoconferencing or higher-speed Internet access.

Digital subscriber line (DSL): Several variations of DSL technology have been developed that provide data rates from 384 kbps or more downstream over existing telephone lines. This technology is replacing ISDN in industrialized countries because of its greater bandwidth. It can be used in urban areas where copper wire is already installed, but its range is limited to about 1 km from a telephone exchange.

Cable modems: Some cable television systems can also be used for high-speed Internet access via cable modems. Like DSL, cable offers much higher bandwidth than dial-up telephone lines. However, a high volume of users may result in congestion of a shared cable network, and older networks may not be converted easily for two-way connectivity.

Optical fiber: Telephone companies upgrading their networks may install optical fiber for institutional customers such as hospitals, schools, and businesses. The advantage of fiber is its enormous bandwidth, which can be used for high-speed Internet accessing or other services such as videoconferencing. However, the price of access may be prohibitive. Some schools have managed to gain free or heavily discounted access to so-called 'dark fiber,' excess capacity that has been installed but is not yet in use.

Hybrid fiber/coax: A combination of optical fiber and coaxial cable can provide broadband services such as TV and high-speed Internet access as well as telephony; this combination is cheaper than installing fiber all the way to the customer premises. Unlike most cable systems, this hybrid allows two-way communication. The fiber runs from a central telephone switch to a neighborhood node; coaxial cable links the node to the end user such as a school. Developing countries with such projects include Chile, China, India, and Malaysia.

Other technological innovations that can be used for educational communication in developing regions include:

Internet telephony (voice over IP): Packetized voice communication can be transmitted very inexpensively over the Internet. Schools with Internet access may be able to use their networks for voice communications as well (regulations vary by country). Using Internet protocols for voice and data is much less expensive than using regular telephone networks.

Community radio: Small community radio broadcasting stations can be important news sources for the community and can be used to broadcast educational radio programs for listening in school, at home, or in community centers. Some school and telecenter projects are combining 89 computer facilities with community radio stations, so that information received via the Internet can be communicated more widely. Portable windup or solar-powered radio receivers are practical for school and community use.

Selecting an Internet Service Provider (ISP): In addition to choosing a means of connecting to the Internet, it also will be necessary to choose an Internet service provider (some ISPs bundle connectivity with services).

Software and Operating Systems

Software, an essential component of computer systems, enables the hardware to do useful work for users. In this section, the discussion about software for educational computer systems is organized into the following four broad categories:

- operating system (OS) software for client and server computers;
- basic computer application software, including software for word processing, spreadsheets, presentations, and graphics;
- educational software applications; and
- Internet-related and -delivered software, including browsers, Java applications, and interactive tools on Websites.

Decisions about what operating system software to use on client or end-user computers are usually based on the type of hardware purchased. If Apple computers are purchased, then Apple's OS, which comes with the computer, will likely be used on client computers. If computers with Intel or Intel-compatible CPUs are purchased, the computers likely will come with a version of the Microsoft Windows OS. In contrast, decisions about what software should be used to operate networked computers are not as easy or predetermined as they are with client system software. Basic Apple and Windows operating system software comes with the capability to enable computers to be connected together to manage small networks. However, larger and more robust networks that may need to be managed securely will require special network operating system software installed on the network's server to manage the functions of the network, including links to printers and other peripherals, e-mail, file sharing, security functions, and communication among linked computers.

There are different options for network operating system software. For Apple computer systems, two main options are available: Apple's own network operating system and Linux. For Intel-based computers, the three main options are Microsoft NT, Novel Netware, and Linux. It is beyond the scope of this chapter to present a detailed comparison of these network operating system software options.

Open Source Software (OSS)

One of the most hotly debated topics in educational technology today deals with the question of whether it is better for school systems to use open source software (OSS) or commercial software products for client and server operating systems. There are no simple answers to this question since they involve policy, commercial, technical, and educational concerns. For education systems, the education functions that need to be supported and the needs of students and teachers are the most important factors in making technology decisions. If the software and hardware solutions do not ultimately serve the teaching and learning process, then even "inexpensive" or "free" options can be very costly educationally. If key educational software programs cannot be used on computer systems with "free" OS software, then the "free" solution could become very expensive. Similarly, educational uses and needs for computers are often quite different from corporate needs—and decision making about technology choices for schools needs to reflect these differences.

Linux, part of the family of UNIX-based operating systems, is one of the most popular open source software products used for computer operating system software. Linux has become popular primarily because it is available free of charge and has a large development and user community. Linux is also the first or second most popular operating system software for Internet servers—accounting for about 30% of all Web servers in the world today. It is used only rarely as a client operating system (on the end terminal or PC at the user's desk), however, mainly because few software applications, such as word processing, can be used on computers running Linux.

The technical benefits of operating system and network operating system software generally are discussed in terms of the software's reliability, performance, scalability, security, and cost. A variety of comparisons have shown that servers running Linux crash less often and perform better than commercial and other OSS software. Also, Linux can be used on a wider range of computer platforms than any other operating system and is more secure than commercial OSS. Finally, studies have shown that Linux and other open source software usually have significantly lower initial costs than commercial operating system software.

Proponents of using Linux in educational computer environments often emphasize the fact that Linux is 'free,' and that the money saved from not having to purchase operating system or network operating system software is a sufficient reason to use it. Unfortunately, this argument is seriously flawed. Operating system and network operating system software only account for about 5% to 8% of the total cost of buying a client computer system. In contrast, the ongoing costs to train teachers to integrate technology into teaching and learning, and to support and keep computer systems running from year to year, can be many times greater than the original purchase cost of the computer and the operating system or network operating system software.

In many cases, school systems will spend as much in two years for operating school computers as was spent initially to purchase and install a system that is expected to last five years. Therefore, it is more important to consider the total cost of ownership carefully—acquiring, installing, configuring, supporting, maintaining, training users in, using, and upgrading the software—when evaluating the real costs of using different types of operating or network operating system software. It is also important to emphasize that total cost of ownership studies carried out for corporations cannot and should not be used to justify purchase decisions for educational systems.

There are special and critical differences between the needs and uses of computers in education and corporations. The most important factor in realizing the potential educational benefits of technology is how teachers and students use computers and the Internet in learning activities. Consequently, the most important cost factors in total cost of ownership studies of technology in education are linked to the use of technology and its integration into teaching and learning. Therefore, when evaluating the use of OSS in education, it is essential to assess how different software decisions will affect how teachers and students use technology and how easy or difficult it may be for them to integrate it into routine teaching and learning.

Windows is the operating system used on 80% to 90% of all client computers in business, government, and the nonprofit sectors of the economy. If students were to use computers in schools with OSS, some likely would not gain the needed skills and experience with Windows that prospective employers would demand. Therefore, total cost of ownership calculations for education systems considering OSS would need to consider the costs that students and companies would likely incur to train workers to use Windows.

The lack of educational software applications that can operate on OSS, and the loss of current investment in Windows applications that could not be used on OSS, without using emulation software, would need to be considered as well in total cost of ownership calculations. Furthermore, many schools, especially those in developing countries, have very small budgets to purchase additional software for their computer systems. A shift to OSS would make some current investments useless, and replacing the software with versions to run on OSS, if they were available, would drain scarce resources. Also, some critical applications, such as software used in special-needs education, are not available for the OSS operating system, and a shift to OSS could prevent some students and schools from using their computers.

When considering the technical specifications of educational computer systems, especially regarding the use of open source software, it is critical that the primary goals and objectives of such systems—significantly improving the quality and equity of teaching and learning—remain the principal focus of decision making. If decisions to use OSS are made for short-term or immediate cost savings, it is possible that the long-term costs, both financially and educationally, may become excessive. The development of total cost of ownership models to assist decision making must reflect unique local realities and include the significant hidden costs associated with building the capacity of educators to integrate the use of computers and the Internet effectively into routine teaching and learning.

Basic Computer Application Software

All computers in schools require a basic set of software applications to be useful for computer literacy programs and to be integrated effectively into routine education programs. These applications generally include software for word processing and manipulating numeric data such as spreadsheets, presentation software, and graphics software, and the increasingly important software to create Websites and HTML documents. As with operating system software, commercial and public domain options are available. Major commercial applications often are purchased because they are the types of software used in businesses and government offices, and it is often important to prepare students to use computers and applications that are common in the workforce. Where funding is a constraint, schools have the option of using Sun Microsystems public domain software application suite, called OpenOffice. It includes an integrated graphical interface similar to MS-Office and WordPerfect and comprises word processing, spreadsheet, and presentation applications. StarOffice also has support for AutoPilot Web page design software, 3D graphics, diagrams, HTML editing, and calendar, newsgroup, browser, e-mail and scheduler, photo editing, and other applications. This software is also available in a variety of languages and can be downloaded for free from the Internet.

Thousands of software applications have been developed over the years, many for free, to meet specific educational objectives, including:

— strengthening subject matter competence;

— providing drill and practice activities for different subjects;

— enhancing logical thinking and problem-solving skills;

— enriching research and writing activities;

— simulating complex or dangerous processes that enable students to change variables and visualize how processes are changed; and

— providing opportunities for students to extend learning beyond the scope of classroom activities.

As with all uses of computers to enhance and improve teaching and learning, the key to success is not the type of educational software that is used, but how teachers use the software and integrate it into their teaching programs. For example, research has shown that when drill and practice software is used without active teacher participation, performance on standardised math tests can go down. In contrast, when this type of software is integrated into a comprehensive set of activities and actively facilitated by teachers, performance on standardized tests can improve.

It is commonly believed that the best educational return on investments in computer systems in schools comes from using specialized educational software. Numerous Websites can provide evaluations of educational software. Also, publishers often will provide evaluation copies of software that teachers can use to test the products before the school decides to purchase them. When evaluating educational software, teachers and schools need to develop evaluation criteria so that purchase decisions are based on objective and subjective measures of educational quality.

One of the most important benefits of Internet- and Web-related software is that most of it can be used regardless of the hardware and software installed at schools. The "platform independence" of the Internet reduces the costs involved in using the Internet in education and enhances its benefits. One key area of Internet use is access to a variety of Internet and Web-based software applications, much of it freely available in different languages that can be used by teachers and students in a variety of ways, including:

— browser and search software that enables students to carry out research on the Internet and engage in enquiry-based learning activities using the millions of Websites on the Internet;

— e-mail software that allows users to send and receive communication from other learners and Websites;

— listserv or e-mail distribution software that allows groups of users to form and communicate easily by e-mail;

— Web-based discussion forum software that allows users to engage in ongoing dialogues in which the topics or themes are linked to form discussion threads;

— interactive Web-based publishing tools that allow students and teachers to publish their thoughts, comments, experiences, pictures, suggestions, etc., instantly on Web pages;

— Internet- and Web-based chat and instant messaging software that allows users to engage in live text-based discussions;

— easy-to-use Web page construction and publishing tools;

— voice and video software applications that allow teachers and students to participate in synchronous audio- and videoconferencing, if sufficient bandwidth is available; and

— file storage and retrieval software that allows users to share digital files easily, including documents, presentations, images, data, and music, with other users.

The existence of these online or Web-based software applications that enable users to communicate at a distance has given rise to opportunities for collaborative and project-based learning that were not possible before the Internet. Since learning is very much a social activity, the ability to link students and teachers together to form learning communities can significantly enhance learning outcomes and opportunities to develop lifelong learning skills.

Another important category of Internet-related software includes applications, many of which are freely available, that enable teachers and students to construct and publish Web pages and HTML documents on the Internet. In addition, the Internet's 'platform independence' helped give rise to a variety of software applications, including JAVA, FLASH, and Shockwave, which can be used to create learning applications that simulate simple and complex processes and concepts. These programming languages can be used by teachers, students, and mediated learning specialists to create simulations that can accelerate understanding of complex concepts and demonstrate scientific activities that normally would need to be carried out in expensive labs.

Carrying out an assessment of needs, physical conditions, constraints and opportunities, and weighting factors, according to their importance, will contribute greatly to deciding which type of configuration optimizes resources against needs. It is also important to examine the capacity of local markets to support different options, especially new, innovative, state-of-the-art technologies. Throughout the information-gathering and decision-making process, it is important to evaluate options and alternatives against the ultimate objective of all school computer systems—to enhance teaching and learning.

Development of Multimedia Materials

Many nations are increasing their investments in education and education technology to support the transformation of teaching and learning. Yet, not enough attention is given to the development and availability of instructional content-ware that makes the investments in hardware economically useful and educationally meaningful.

One possible reason is that equipping schools with radios, televisions, and computers and connecting them to the Internet is simple compared to developing corresponding instructional materials. For a visual artist about to create a new work, the choice of medium is a question of supreme importance. Each medium carries within it a certain relationship to the gesture, a demand for restraint, limitations of texture, hue, value, plasticity.

For the educationist, the term, 'multimedia,' has become much more definite. It signals high cost, a simplistic blend of visual and aural information, and low return.

Today multimedia as a means of learning is equated with tightly structured content built by a commercial vendor—a developer. It is a product, not a possibility. The excitement of choice, of trial, of process is absent. Yet, multimedia in its broadest sense is among the most effective and egalitarian of computer-based resources available. By establishing the potential for the artful interaction between learners and content—intertwining information, skills, and even the synthesizing vision that is so important to comprehension—multimedia 'contentware' is effective across the wide range of circumstances.

Multimedia can be designed to:

— enhance learning in different locations and in schools of diverse quality;

— present opportunities for students working at different rates and levels;

— provide (tirelessly, without holding up other students) repetition when repetition is warranted to reinforce skills and learning; and

— compensate, in the short term, for high student populations and limited numbers of trained and experienced teachers—in combination with robust teacher development initiatives and improvements in teachers' working conditions.

In dynamic fields, such as astrophysics, genetics, or political geography, updates to contentware can ensure that teachers and students encounter and have the chance to work with current and even cutting-edge knowledge. Such encounters tie learning to the most important events of our time and underscore the general idea that knowledge itself is not fixed and finalized, that there is a universe of discoveries and a library of analyses that can be available to students.

Finally, computer-based and Web-based multimedia content-ware is itself dynamic, built of bits and bytes, using software development tools that combine, in some cases, the power to create with the simplicity of use. Unlike textbooks or library-based resources, contentware has the potential to engage all stakeholders in the education system—from software developers to ministry personnel to education researchers to teachers and students—in the development of multimedia learning resources.

A decade and more ago, national efforts to introduce ICTs in education anticipated increases in efficiency, without attending to the nature of learning and cognition, or to the distinction between skills mastered in abstraction and knowledge built to be used, expanded, and eventually transcended. To build resources that enable learners to build knowledge, we must broaden our perspective beyond building skills and memorizing facts in the abstract; if these are our educational goals, technology will prove neither cost-effective nor effective in absolute terms. If our goals include enhancing analysis, synthesis, communication, and the grasping of interrelationships in the ways in which we represent our world, we will find that technology supports and empowers all of our efforts along these lines.

The use of multimedia as engines of learning is conditioned by several dynamic contexts, including our relevant to student experience. To accomplish this objective, multimedia development must consider cognitive complexity, sensitivity to instruction, meaningfulness, reliability, fairness, and linguistic appropriateness.

Multimedia material produced for teaching and learning must be produced for assessment as well, with compatible goals, similar depth, and equal quality.

When developing educational multimedia resources, it is important to take into account objectives at the level of the individual learner, the school, and the state. Each has different characteristics, expectations, and needs, and the means to fulfill them are all interrelated. For this reason, development of learning resources is linked, strategically, with processes of educational reform and the transformation of teaching and learning. Thus, the suggest four points of focus for planning the development of multimedia educational material.

Technology also may enable us to support these goals through a combination of preauthoring (i.e., design) tools, classroom work, portfolio-organization systems, publication systems, and collaboration tools. In such an environment, the most useful multimedia material might be small bits and pieces of software that are plugable and insertable in student's pages perhaps allowing user customizations. In this environment, students are motivated not only by the drive for visual quality in their work, but by the opportunity to use and discuss material that they, working independently in the classroom-based learning environment, would be unable to produce on their own.

The emergence of technology as a change factor in education coincides with the sweeping influence of cognitive science and brain studies as a factor in the transformation of teaching and learning.

The influence of both of these forces has increased with the recognition of globalization, the concomitant demonstrations of the value of innovation, and the prevalence of strong "knowledge-work" sectors.

Beyond thinking skills, thinking dispositions are important—students must have sensibility to know when and how to apply their skills. Development of such competencies can be fostered by the creation of a culture of thinking in the classroom. In this way students are able to develop successful strategies to transfer their learning to other situations. From these concepts about learning, and more recently from discussion of the skill sets needed in the "global, knowledge economy," new pedagogical rubrics have emerged that include cooperative learning, collaborative learning, active learning, problem-based learning, situated learning and, most recently, 'learning by doing.'

These approaches all aim at a transfer of emphasis away from rote-based methods and assessment, and the teacher as the "producer" of knowledge. Instead, they emphasize the roles that analysis, synthesis, and other higher-order cognitive skills play in learning, with particular focus on learners building their own knowledge. Expanding view of multimedia must also take into account multimedia examination formats.

Students and faculty feel that incorporation of rich media in assessment can provide additional support for learning and teaching. Advances in technology, cognitive science, and measurement also show the need to reinvent large-scale assessment, and this process of reinvention may stand to benefit from incorporation of multimedia.

Technology can play a crucial role in connecting schools to professionals in their communities and around the world, and by allowing the school to develop ideas and positions and make them public.

Many students are motivated to include high-quality material in their projects and pages. With access to appropriate data-bases of educational and multimedia resources they can search, modify, and combine such material to use in their presentations and explanations. Clearly, there are no boundaries among these four focal areas. When construct an assessment-centered learning environment, we create elements of a learner-centered environment. When we build a community-centered environment, satisfy criteria for a knowledge-centered environment. Well-designed systems combine characteristics of all four.

Nature and Modalities of Multimedia

Content can be presented to learners using tools ranging from books and lectures to the Internet or even handheld computers. Each different instrument—whether a book or a handheld—communicates its content in one or more modes. A book, for example, readily accommodates text, of course, plus images that can range from line drawings to schematics to maps to photographs. These modalities and instruments offer different 'affordances' (or features that facilitate a specific type of interaction).

Text, as a mode for content presentation, can present complex information, although it requires literacy, analytical, and mnemonic skills. As an instrument for text-based content presentation, books are portable and easy to read, guide sequential reading, and do not require electricity. It also can help in enabling learners to reframe knowledge. Multimedia also can broaden the scope of school learning environments by enabling experiments that otherwise would be too dangerous, too expensive, or take too long. And visualization and modeling tools give students the opportunity to enter into much more complex knowledge-contexts, while continuing to build their comprehension of the core knowledge of those domains.

Multimedia offers the opportunity to combine instruments and modes to radically enhance the effectiveness of learning resource development efforts. Educational publishers frequently 'bundle' CD-ROMs with textbooks, providing additional resources, updates, and other information. Interactive simulations are often 'wrapped' with text addressed directly to learners, providing contextualizing information, and with text addressed to teachers guiding them in facilitation of classroom activities, questioning strategies, and assessment. In this sense, supporting radio broadcasts or audiocassettes with print-based workbooks comprises a multimedia combination of different instruments. In all of these combinations, not only are limitations mitigated, but the strengths of each instrument are also magnified beyond the potential of any single instrument deployed in isolation. The characteristic implies a fundamental goal of multimedia design—to combine instruments in ways that best address the requirements of a specific content domain, the abilities and deficits of targeted learners, and the infrastructure and systemic conditions of the prospective learning environment to achieve results beyond what is possible with individual instruments and isolated media.

The Internet and CD-ROMs, of course, have the potential to serve as platforms for the full range of modes—text, images, audio, video, and simulations. To this potential, the Internet adds the possibility of frequent updates, collaborative or participatory solutions, and near-infinite scalability. Bandwidth and platform constraints, however, continue to pose limits in most circumstances. In all instances, effective design and development processes are required to arrive at a creative, effective, and appropriate implementation that addresses specific parameters.

Educational gains can be maximized for every situation when the most appropriate tools are used. It is not possible, however, to give recipes for what technology tools to use or when to use them. Each case is distinct. In such cases, it is also important to keep in mind the infrastructure or pedagogical constraints that may impede effective use of such multimedia.

Videos motivate students by showing real-life situations, in ways that are often superior to a teacher narrating them or a text describing them. Videos can be used when they do require light of some sort). They offer a balance between their ability to present large quantities of content—through both text and images—and the reader's ability to build an overview of the entire body of content—based on indexes, chapter headings, and other explicit structuring—to discover the most relevant material. A Web page, which also presents information via text and images, is easier to modify and can be linked to many other pages to provide different pathways through the text.

Each modality and instrument offers specific affordances in combination with specific limitations. In addition, factors such as design, construction, development, and support vary among specific resources of a given type. In addition, external factors, such as a region's technical infrastructure, its climate, overall education system, and even the health and nutrition of individual learners, will determine the degree to which a resource's affordances are realized and its limitations minimized. Current major modalities for content presentation are text, images, audio, video, and simulations. Each of these modalities can be presented via many instruments. The information presented is intended to provide an overall picture of modalities and instruments only, not to enable absolute rankings. Specific designs and implementations should be analyzed relative to the objectives they are intended to support and the environments in which they will be deployed.

Affordances can be optimized and limitations minimized for a given instrument in a specific implementation through appropriate design and development. In a multiplatform environment, for example, in which early- and late-model PCs are mixed with Macintosh computers, interactive simulations can be written in Java to provide multiplatform interoperability. In low-bandwidth environments, requirements for plug-ins such as Flash Player can be avoided, or CD-ROMs can be used as the primary delivery instrument. Introducing a new theme to motivate and contextualize learning, after a topic has been addressed in a few class periods to aid students in applying the knowledge they acquired, or after an entire module is completed to show connections to other subjects and disciplines.

Video production is not easy. If a video is intended for widespread use or for broadcast, required resources and resulting costs mount quickly. Professionals should be involved in production of good storyboards, lighting and shooting the video, and editing and postproduction. Beta-for-mat equipment should be used, rather than VHS, to ensure high quality. Videos produced for viewing on computers are somewhat different; resolution can be low, and it should be low for most platforms currently in schools. Such videos may be displayed to large groups via multimedia projector, or individually or in small groups on individual computer work-stations.

The Digital Video Disc (DVD) format brings benefits to schools in terms of storage and durability; however, most schools do not have DVD players, and care must be taken in all cases to ensure compatibility of disc formats and players. Short videos present a whole new arena. High-compression formats such as MPEG, RealVideo, ASF, and QuickTime are suitable for delivery over the Web or by CD-ROM, and plug-in players for these formats are available as free downloads from the Internet. Short videos can be integrated into computer activities in labs or computer-equipped classrooms. They can demonstrate dramatic effects or experiments that are too costly or dangerous to be performed in schools. Production of Web- or CD-ready videos can be accomplished through relatively low-cost processes, in labs or in the open air using a camcorder, with a robust computer workstation equipped with a video card, used for editing. Specialists are not necessary.

Internet service provision, and school hardware) is a key factor for transmitting them. In addition, storage space and storage media can be problematic. Older computers, especially, may lack both hard drive space and processing power to run videos—and student workstations of all vintages generally lack hard drive space sufficient to store videos in any quantity. Complementary distribution of videos, via DVD, CD-ROMs, or VHS tapes, can address Internet- and computer-related problems. It can be effective to integrate time-sensitive information—such as news, student work, and so on—with large media resources, such as videos, distributed on fixed media.

Audio technology has been used widely with tape recorders and radio programs. Some uses do not depend on the production of material, but stem, instead, from good infrastructure. For instance, students can progress rapidly in language studies if they interact with students from other places; they can hear specific and authentic dialects and languages. Advanced consumer tools that support these activities include Internet Protocol Telephony (I.P. Phone), CUseeMe, and NetMeeting. In addition, the explosive popularity of various techniques for exchanging music over the Internet has already led many students to explore the power of information exchange via Web-based and peer-to-peer collaboration.

Many students are eager to produce and publish their own sound files. It is easy to channel such motivated activity toward production of materials that also have educational value—for the creator. Again, resource considerations may pose limitations: although software is not too expensive, it is necessary to have a good sound card, a good processor, and sufficient RAM (random access memory) and storage capacity. Maybe the most interesting materials that can be produced are those that explore sound and image at the same time.

The most remarkable aspect of simulations is interactivity, or the opportunity for the learner to change values or conditions and see what happens. This capability motivates students to formulate and test hypotheses. Simulations represent the temporal dimension visually and experientially, making them different from images, text, sound, and video. In some cases, they can enhance experiences gained in real school science labs by allowing virtual experimentation in ideal conditions. The realism of these conditions can be increased gradually. Simulations also can enable experimentation with concepts that cannot be experimented with in actual school-based labs.

In particular, development of CD-ROM-based stand-alone suites that use interactive simulations as substitutes for school science labs tends to lead to overly complex and machine-straining products, although worthy exceptions do exist. One easy means of presenting simulations to students is to position them on "html" pages that can be served to the Internet. All computation then runs in the browser, making the simulation itself generally easy to run on any recent combination of hardware and software. However, some Java-based simulations are large and memory-intensive and cannot be run on older machines with limited processor speed and memory. It is possible, when these situations are anticipated, to run calculations in the server and transmit only data to the browser—although in these instances, bandwidth constraints and network configurations simply shift the problem to another area. Flash and Shockwave output is easy to create and often "runs light"; however, their programming languages are not as robust as Java, and these files may not run across a range of platforms. Among the difficulties with CD-ROM-delivered simulations is cost, which may be high, based on the number of licenses required for an entire class or lab.

Problems also can arise from complex or time-consuming installation procedures, complex design, and lack of technical and pedagogical support. Again, solutions to some of these challenges involve centralization of computing power and administration through client-server systems based at the lab, school, or district level.

Animations

Animations stand in contrast with videos and simulations: they do not use real images, nor do they enable interaction with the learner. Despite these significant constraints, animations are very powerful, especially as a means of enhancing otherwise static images—whether in textbooks or on Web pages. Animations can be used to motivate learning, demonstrate concepts, and, as tools, emphasize particular details or aspects of complex phenomena. Animations often may be the best tools for highlighting the path between modeling and reality. It is possible to create a sequence of visualizations with increasing degrees of sophistication, enabling student understanding to go far beyond crude and simple models. Animations are created by digitizing and sequencing hand-drawn images, or directly through the use of 3-D and other software. As we have seen with other media, older computers with limited memory and slow processors have problems with animations generated by 3-D software because these are usually large and heavy.

Private-sector activities in multimedia development can also be extremely varied. Whereas private-sector activity for much of the 1990s focused on development of

CD-ROM-based multimedia, with mixed results in terms of both educational and financial success, more recent activity has explored a range of models involving the Internet. Innovation has come, sporadically, when smaller companies have launched products that have focused on student creativity (e.g., HyperStudio), and when they have based development on a solid foundation of learning research.

In countries in which institutional or national organizations have not yet established education portals, private companies have rushed to fill that gap. In the United States, has emerged as the premier aggregator of education resources and services, offering a catalog of lesson plans, productivity resources for students and teachers that include professional Web-construction tools, career and professional development resources for teachers, and a host of other resources. Because many of the lesson plans and student projects have been developed outside of the bigchalk organization, these tend to be heterogeneous, although efforts have been made to cover broad areas of the common curriculum in the United States, and to ensure that resources meet bigchalk's standards of quality.

Challenges to Private-Sector Authorship

When private-sector development of effective CD-ROM-based educational materials has been successful, as in the case of the Cognitive Tutor, success has come despite structural factors, chiefly economic, that have tended to limit the effectiveness of resources created by centralized development. It may be instructive to review those factors historically and their effects, in part to determine their continuing effect on centralized development—for both CDs and the Internet. Chief among these factors, of course, is the persistently high cost of software development, with an average for educational CDs reported to be US$400,000 in 1994.

Pressures of this sort force private-sector developers to design education products for the broadest possible audience, including not only teachers and students in state schools and private schools, but also families, students using computers at home, and, in some cases, private test-preparation and tutoring companies. The nonschool segments of the developers' market base may prove to be larger and more easily reached by marketing efforts, and the decision to purchase may be made more easily. However, the various learning environments—school labs, after-school labs, and homes—provide learners with radically different circumstances. The one-learner/one-computer configuration implied in the design of most commercially produced education software is rarely provided in a school classroom or lab. And these designs fail to support—and may actually interfere with—the essential social aspects of learning.

With low profit margins and little incentive to develop "school-only" titles, developers have little reason to assume the risks of innovation. As evidence, the Cognitive Tutor product line was recognized in 1999 by the U.S. Department of Education as one of only five of 61 available math software products as "exemplary"—after more than 10 years of multimedia development by the private sector (Eisenhower National Clearinghouse). In 1999, the Turkish Ministry of National Education rejected all bids from software developers to a tender that was part of its Basic Education Project, spanning 8,000 schools, because none of the products met their requirements.

Teacher Developers and Collaborative Efforts Due in part to the challenges confronting private-sector developers—and in part to changes in pedagogical approaches—teachers in many countries have been seen as partners in and even drivers of development of technology-based learning resources over the past 10 years. During the early years of multimedia development in the United States, classroom teachers drove the start-up of education software 106 companies such as Minnesota Educational Computing Corporation (MECC), Sunburst, the Learning Company, and many others. Although its tools are solidly grounded in cognitive science, Carnegie Learning has incorporated the results of extensive field trials of its Cognitive Tutor line conducted by William Hadley, 1995's U.S. Math Teacher of the Year. Although these companies benefit from the teachers' experience and knowledge, they are constrained by market-based pressures. New tools and new understanding of the value of the teacher's experience have combined to generate new processes to develop multimedia learning resources. Apple Computer's 1984 introduction of HyperCard gave perhaps the first promise of software learning resources developed by working teachers, and today we see teachers developing Web-based resources. Three projects initiated in the late 1990s explore teachers' potential as collaborators in resource development:

— The Educational Object Economy (EOE),

— Multimedia Educational Resource for Learning and Online Teaching (MERLOT), and

— Educational Software Objects of Tomorrow (ESCOT).

— The Educational Object Economy (EOE)

The EOE emerged out of a 1993 NSF grant to the East/ West Authoring Tools Group, a coalition of universities and publishers anchored by Apple Computer's Advanced Technology Group. The initial objective of the grant was to sponsor development of menu-driven "end-user" authoring tools that could reduce the high cost of multimedia CD-ROM development. However, the met with unanticipated difficulties with the repurposing of university-built tools for commercial uses. At the same time, the emerging dominance of both the Internet and Sun's Java scripting language pointed to the decreasing importance of CD-ROM-based delivery.

The success of subsequent efforts to enable authoring tools to generate Java output led to a crucial realization—without coordinating mechanisms, a proliferation of authors and authoring tools leads to redundant development of the "low-hanging fruit" of software resources. In 1997, the Educational Object Economy launched a dynamic, database-served Website as a place where users could post interactive simulations constructed as Java applets. These small, Web-delivered simulations generally enable learners to change variables and see the results of their changes graphically and quantitatively.

Lifted by waves of interest in both Java and the Internet, and in open-source development models, the EOE now features over 2,000 Java-based simulations for education. Applets have been developed and contributed freely by teachers, students, programmers, and education researchers, with meta-data that include reviews, comments, and curriculum-based activities, as well as catalog information based on an early version of the Instructional Management System (IMS) model. In roughly one-quarter of these applets, Java source code is available for modification and localization.

Globalization affects every sector involved in education development; from the largest education portals to private and even homespun efforts. Again, internationalization is most effective when it is planned in advance, and when the foundation for translation and localization is included in development frameworks and processes. In principle, everything that is text-based is easily translated. Problems occur, however, with text contained in images, animations, and simulations. In these cases, not only the translator but also the designer or programmer must participate in implementing a translation. However, newly available tools and technologies enable textual elements, such as component labels in the graphical user interface, to be stored outside the source code and retrieved dynamically.

Open-source educational software is available on the Internet, much of it in the form of Java-based simulations. However, in some instances, projects have begun in very open modes and then have found it necessary to restrict use and access to achieve sustainability or increased control over the use of resources. The ExploreScience and ExploreMath sites are wonderful examples of the use of simulations to foster learning. In the early stages of these sites, visitors to them could download simulations onto their hard drives for use offline—a necessary feature in many schools with poor Internet access or other infrastructure limitations. New resources developed for these sites, however, can only be run over a "live" Internet connection, although it is still possible to follow links to a classic version of the site that offers older resources in compressed, downloadable versions. There are other examples in which restrictions have been applied after projects have been launched. Early versions of the applets produced in this project were accessible and were excellent examples of good coding. However, the code for these resources is no longer available. This is a typical case of noncommercial use that could very well benefit from a GPL license. Many educational portals have begun by offering free access, and then have shifted to fee-based access. Biology Labs Online, which contains interactive, inquiry-based biology simulations and exercises, started by offering free access to the first labs. Now, however, visitors to the site receive three days' free access, for trial purposes, after which a subscription is required.

Multimedia resources—considered in terms of both products and processes—have great potential to enhance education. New modalities and instruments for development and delivery have radically increased the support that these resources can give students across a wide range of learning activities. Despite the glamour of technology-rich environments, focus must remain on learners and their motivations and challenges, on the knowledge domains to be explored, and on the communities in which learning will take place. We also must keep in mind that developers, teachers, and students all have roles to play in the creation of multimedia, and one of the chief goals of policy must be to support appropriate activities by each of these groups. Flexibility is a key property of multimedia contentware, and must be marshaled effectively in our development efforts. Despite the complexity of their interaction, the contexts for development and implementation—cognitive, instructional, and technological—can be balanced so as to advance strategic goals and plans within our education systems.

Cognitive science, in particular, can guide and give shape to innovation in the development of learning environments, multimedia resources, and teaching and learning practice. Both institutional and private-sector developers can draw on advances in learning science to design innovative and effective contentware.

Globalisation and Higher Education

Higher education is now a major element on the international agenda. The organisations such as United Nations Educational, Scientific & Cultural Organisation (UNESCO), the World Bank and the Organisation for Economic Co-operation and Development (OECD) acknowledge the crucial role for education in economic development throughout the world. In these reports the roles for higher education in economic development, the globalisation of the world economy, the development of a knowledge-based society and the education and training of a skilled and flexible workforce are seen as crucial.

Academic and academic related staff in higher education are increasingly likely to become involved in a variety of ways in educational activities with an international dimension whether as policy makers, advisors, members of research or teaching groups or as individual practitioners. This increasing international participation has had the effect of both emphasising existing problems of ethical issues arising out of academic work and of raising new ones; there is growing concern expressed as more examples of unethical behaviour are made public. This section is intended to identify some of the issues that might arise and to set them within the context of values shared by the Association of University Teachers (AUT) and the Development and Education Association (DEA) in order to provide a framework within which practitioners can identify and address ethical questions arising out of their activities.

There are seldom quick and straightforward answers to ethical dilemmas. This document cannot and does not attempt to address all the possible issues which may arise when university staff are contemplating or engaged in international work. In developing the document attention has been paid to roles university staff may be called upon to play in international academic activities; in particular, those arising from recruitment and teaching of and support of overseas students and from collaboration with overseas institutions through franchising arrangements and research which either draws on material from other countries and/or involves collaboration with colleagues overseas. With these activities in mind, further consideration is then given to two areas where it is felt ethical issues are most likely to be presented in a university environment which is becoming increasingly competitive and driven to secure 'commercial' income—human rights and environmental sustainability. It is the premise of this document that principles underlining these two issues, while not uncontroversial, are nevertheless fundamental to a notion of academic professionalism and the idea of the 'role of service' generally held by those concerned with the provision of higher education.

Against this background the section sets out to:

1. raise awareness of increasing potential for ethical dilemmas resulting from the increased role of universities in a global market;
2. provide both background information on areas of possible ethical concern and on sources of information which can assist practitioners in determining their own ethical stance; and
3. set an agenda for considered policy development for the AUT and universities to establish frameworks for resolving potential ethical concerns, which avoid such issues having to be resolved by individual members of staff without any institutional support.

Perceptions of the Role of Higher Education

Perceptions of the proper responses of higher education policy makers and practitioners to contemporary international trends may be very different. Some commentators see higher education narrowly defined as serving largely economic goals:

There is consistent evidence from multiple sources of a strong positive relationship between educational attainment levels and output and productivity growth. New Challenges - Lifelong Learning to Maintain Employability, OECD. Others regard it more broadly as part of a process of lifelong learning that both prepares citizens to contribute economically to society and but also to contribute ethically, culturally, socially and politically.

There is a need to rethink and broaden the notion of lifelong education. Not only must it adapt to changes in the nature of work but it also constitutes a continuous process of forming whole human beings - their knowledge and aptitudes, as well as the critical faculty and ability to act. It should enable people to develop awareness of themselves and their environment and encourage them to play their social role at work and in the community.

Higher education should reinforce its role of service to society, especially in assisting eliminating poverty, intolerance, violence, illiteracy, hunger, environmental degradation and disease. Reinforced links with the world of work with efforts devoted to developing students' entrepreneurial skills so that they become job creators as well as job seekers.

National and institutional decision-makers should place students and their needs at the centre of their concerns greater sharing of knowledge and expertise across national borders and the need to stem the brain drain, with priority given to training programmes in the developing countries, in centres of excellence forming regional and international networks, with short periods of specialised and intensive study abroad.

While accepting that higher education is now a multi-million pound export earner, the AUT takes the position that the sector's mission as a provider of quality education, research and training must not be compromised. The global marketing of higher education means that academic staff may be called upon to weigh professional and ethical principles against financial imperatives. AUT recognises that there are no easy or universal answers, but it believes that members will find it timely to consider these issues and their own positions with respect to them. The DEA, as well as believing that wider world issues and perspectives should be an integral feature of all educational activity, holds that a commitment to equity, social justice and sustainable development should underpin all educational policies and initiatives.

Development education is concerned with the quality of teaching and learning, the ethos of the learning environment and the democratic participation of learners and the learning process. Development education places importance on problem posing as much as upon problem solving, on the application of interpretive and resolutive skills as much as upon the acquisition of knowledge, on the local as much as upon the global and on Northern as much as upon Southern development, arguing that the world is best viewed as an interactive whole.

Higher Education in a Global Society

Toward this end three themes are explored here, international partnerships and activities, human rights, and sustainable development. The AUT appreciates that many academics are eager to engage with sustainable development, to strengthen democratic institutions and practices and to contribute to a fairer distribution of global rewards and resources. A substantial number are already engaged in what the UNESCO conference called higher education's 'role of service' and they take such work very seriously indeed. Approaches to education, research and training that fail to reconcile the social and the environmental with the economic are increasingly seen as flawed. World Bank thinking is firmly disposed to the view that improvement of the human condition and the preservation of the environment are inseparable from education and training for sustainable and democratic development:

> The Bank helps to facilitate learning and strengthen client country capacity through EDI's activities (the Economic Development Institute). As greater emphasis has been placed upon knowledge as a catalyst of reform, EDI has launched and piloted core courses on development priorities from banking, finance and regulation to environment and sustainable development and from governance to human and social development.

Tony Blair Speech at the 53rd UN General Assembly, New York:

> If higher education allows itself to be dominated by competition and financial interests, it runs the risk of intellectual isolation. Knowledge may be generated but not distributed unless it is paid for. To reach the appropriate audiences academics need to incorporate professional, ethical and financial systems of quality assurance in the planning, monitoring, evaluation and review of entrepreneurial activity.

The DEA has a strategy group looking at how global and development education perspectives can be eflected within all aspects of higher education activity. This includes working with a range of non-governmental organisations who are engaged in educational and awareness raising projects with students and academics, a joint initiative with Forum for the Future and organising a series of seminars with appropriate research centres on the impact of globalisation and international development on educational programmes in the developing countires.

There are so many sources of support and guidance available that it would be a major enterprise to list them all. However, members may find the following helpful.

— university charters and statutes

— terms of reference of university committees dealing with ethics and professional standards

— professional and ethical obligations (e.g. conditions for membership to professional bodies)

— contracts of employment, terms and conditions of service and other associated documents

— codes of practice on international collaboration and guidelines for working with overseas students.

— documentation from special interest organisations.

— national and international documents

Human Rights

The Universal Declaration of Human Rights is as significant today as it was in 1948 when it was drawn up and ratified by the United Nation's then 58 country members. As UN membership has grown to its present 185 member states, increasing numbers of the world's people have turned to the Declaration to legitimate claims to rights and protest infringements of liberties. This has set in train a process which has enabled us to deepen our understanding of the social, political, economic and cultural interdependence of the nature of human rights and freedoms. The early civil and political emphasis of the Declaration has been expanded to give greater prominence to 'second generation' rights, such as social and cultural rights, which have been augmented over the past decade by 'third generation' rights such as the right to development, to self-determination and to a sustainable environment. Our conception of entitlement to rights has expanded, as has our capacity to perceive how the rights of particular groups (such as children, women, religious and racial minorities and indigenous peoples) require special attention affirmed rights were universal for all peoples regardless of race, religion or country.They had no time for the notion that human rights are subject to any kind of cultural relativism and nor should we fifty years later.

Those fifty years have also left threadbare the excuse that human rights are a luxury which cannot be afforded by countries that are poor. Human rights are indeed of little value without freedom from hunger, from want and from disease. And economic and social rights are as important as civil and political rights. But the past two decades have repeatedly demonstrated that political freedom and economic development are not in conflict, but are mutually reinforcing. Countries with the strongest authoritarian rule are more often than not countries whose economies have stagnated as backwaters in a global economy that has passed them by.

Conversely, the World Bank has concluded that the economies with the faster growth were those where political equality has produced the fairest shares of income. Speech at the Amnesty International Human Rights Festival, London Rights fundamental to academic freedom It could be argued that all rights are fundamental to academic freedom, but this is too broad to provide the practising academic with an adequate reflective focus. The Universal Declaration of Human Rights contains a number of Articles that academics are likely to find particularly relevant:

> Article 18 Everyone has the right to freedom of thought, conscience and religion Article 19 Everyone has the right to freedom of freedom of opinion and

> expression Article 20 (1) Everyone has the right to freedom of peaceful assembly and association Article 23 (4) Everyone has the right to form and to join trade unions for the protection of (her) his interests Article 26 (1) Everyone has the right to education...higher education shall be equally accessible to all on the basis of merit Article 26 (2) Education shall be directed to the full development of the human personality and to the strengthening of respect for human rights and fundamental freedoms Article 27 (1) Everyone has the right freely to participate in the cultural life of the community, to enjoy the arts and to share in scientific advancement and its benefits In addition to the Universal Declaration there are a number of specialist human rights conventions. Academics who work with children, young people and families should refer to the UN Convention on the Rights of the Child (1989). Academics concerned with trade union activities, labour studies and indigenous and tribal peoples should refer to the relevant Internatoinal Labour Office (ILO) Conventions. Knowing which countries have signed up to particular conventions can be as important as knowing what conventions exist. Amnesty International Reports provide a detailed picture of the ratification and accession process of many UN and ILO conventions (and list Amnesty offices and actions worldwide), but the following summary gives us a helpful overview of the process.

The United States has not ratified the conventions on the rights of the child, the elimination of discrimination against women and economic, social and cultural rights. Switzerland and Afghanistan have not acceded to the convention on women. Just over half of the UN's members have signed up to the convention against torture and other cruel, inhuman or degrading punishment, although Indonesia, Nicaragua, Nigeria, Sierra Leone and Belgium are among the objectors.

Whether as actors in the UK higher education system or as members of international academic ventures we find that we are increasingly confronted by difficult ethical decisions. The marketisation of the UK higher education system, with its attendant pressures of exporting courses and intellectual products to other parts of the world, of winning overseas students from competitor universities, and of securing lucrative research contracts from foreign governments and the commercial world, makes academics' roles and responsibilities ever more complex. What follows is based upon the premise that it is better to anticipate and prepare for ethical dilemmas than to respond in a piecemeal way when the storm clouds break. The remainder of the human rights section of this document can be used for personal reflection, though it has to be said that individual members of staff are likely to feel vulnerable if they do not have the shelter of a wider policy umbrella.

This section has considered the role of higher education in an increasingly inter-connected world, a role which is becoming more and more recognised and integrated into the process of economic development. It has also sought to look at development in broader terms than just economic and in a way that reflects higher education's traditional roles and values. While this process may generate apparent tensions, the document seeks to advise on means of managing such tensions. It is indisputable that the world as a whole must develop on a sustainable basis and in a way which seeks to ensure its free and fair enjoyment by all, both present and future generations. Not withstanding the need to respect cultural diversity, increased interaction creates the need to seek global acceptance of fundamental rights, in particular, through educational opportunities.

Furthermore, higher education cannot shirk its responsibilities to human progress and the immediate need to attack world problems of poverty, illiteracy and disease.

These principles must underpin the universities' mission statements and inform the practice of all organisations both within and outside higher education. This document seeks to make such aims explicit and to raise awareness to ensure that universities contribute to them. The information contained in this document should be used by members, local associations and institutions as a basis for critical assessment of the international role of activities of universities and their staff in a manner which places the fundamental issues identified here at the centre of our concerns.

5

ICTs in Teaching and Learning

The present chapter intends to discuss the development and use of information and communication technology (ICT) to support and enhance teaching and learning in colleges of further education. In recent years, colleges have recognised the potential of ICT to support students' learning, to increase participation rates in education and to improve efficiency. They are also aware that ICT is a cost-effective way to contribute to the concept of lifelong learning and to encourage students to develop the skills of independent learning. As a result, colleges have made substantial investments in the development of ICT provision.

Over the past five years, the further education sector has experienced considerable change. To study the changes in detail, let us take the example of further education system of United Kingdom. In that country a survey was undertaken by the Education and Training Inspectorate during the 1998/99 academic year. The findings were very interesting.

In UK, during 1994, the number of further education colleges reduced from 24 to 17 through the merger of 12 colleges to form five new institutions. In 1997, all colleges gained corporate status and became self-governing organisations with responsibility for the use of public funds. The legislation which gives effect to the self-governance of colleges places a requirement on colleges to produce a College Development Plan (CDP) on an annual basis. The Strategic Plan for the Education Service published in May 1996 sets out a number of key objectives and targets for the Education Service, including the further education sector.

The self-governance of colleges has encouraged the development of a competitive market environment in which each college must manage its resources effectively and efficiently to help it achieve its strategic aims. In recent years, there have been significant developments in the further education curriculum which comprises a wide range of courses from basic education to higher education level. National Vocational Qualifications (NVQs) and General National Vocational Qualifications (GNVQs) have replaced many traditional qualifications at craft and technician levels. The further education sector is now expected to make a significant contribution towards the achievement of the National Education and Training Targets through new approaches to learning, including the use of ICT.

In addition, the Government's strategic aim of developing a new culture of lifelong learning throughout Northern Ireland presents an major challenge to the further education sector. The further education sector comprises 17 colleges which vary considerably in size. Many colleges have multiple sites and draw students from a wide geographical area. The largest college has approximately 22,000 students enrolled on a wide range of vocational and academic courses from basic education to higher education levels. In contrast, the smallest college has 650 students enrolled on a range of specialist vocational courses.

In 1997/98, there were approximately 86,000 students enrolled in the colleges. Over the past five years, the total student enrolments have increased by approximately 8%.

The objectives of the programme were to:

— investigate the context influencing the development and use of ICT in the further education sector;

— evaluate the range and quality of ICT provision across all colleges of further education;

— evaluate the effectiveness of ICT in supporting and improving the quality of teaching and learning across a range of vocational and academic areas.

In preparation for the survey, all colleges completed a questionnaire to provide information on the range and quality of the ICT provision and on the arrangements for students to access ICT. The ICT provision covered computer hardware and software, networks and communication systems, audio and video-based systems and specialist computer-based learning centres. Approximately 150 classes ranging from basic education to higher national levels were inspected in eight vocational areas; these were art and design, business, computing, construction, engineering, health and social care, leisure and tourism, and science. In addition, classes in five academic subject areas at GCSE and GCE A level were inspected; these were English, geography, history, mathematics, and modern languages.

The provision for students on community education and basic skills programmes and for students with learning difficulties and disabilities was also inspected. Samples of students' work were reviewed and examples of good practice were identified. Discussions were held with students and staff and senior management who have responsibility for ICT.

The ratio of full-time equivalent students to computers varies considerably between colleges. It ranges from 3:1 to 12:1 with an average of 8:1. Across all colleges, only 37% of computers are up-to-date with comprehensive multimedia facilities. About 40% are around two years old. The remainder are well over two years of age and are used to support a limited range of teaching and learning approaches. One large college has a college-wide network infrastructure. Six colleges have partially integrated and advanced network facilities in place, and the remainder have limited networking capability.

Although all colleges have access to the Internet, the connectivity varies considerably from one to three hundred computer systems. Nine colleges have less than five Internet connection points. Access to computer systems is generally good in 13 colleges. In four colleges access to computers is restricted to timetabled classes for information technology (IT).

Open access to the Internet is provided by four colleges. In the remainder, access is restricted to timetabled classes. The senior management in approximately half the colleges are highly committed to the development and use of ICT to support teaching and learning. They have devised appropriate written policies and strategies aimed at promoting the effective use of educational technology and the concept of lifelong learning. The development of suitable policies and strategies for ICT is at an early stage in about one-fifth of colleges. In about half of the colleges, project groups have worked well to identify the roles and responsibilities of staff, curriculum and staff development needs, and the organisational changes needed to manage ICT successfully across all programme areas.

Approximately one-third of the colleges have not produced written policies or strategies for the development of ICT across the curriculum. As a result, there is no effective planning to use ICT to support teaching and learning, and the development of existing ICT facilities varies considerably between curriculum areas. About three-quarters of the colleges have established procedures, including codes of conduct, to ensure students use the ICT facilities safely and correctly. About three-quarters of the colleges have established common standards for hardware and software. The quality of the technical support for maintenance of the ICT facilities varies considerably across and within the colleges. About half the colleges rely on non-specialist technicians and have difficulty in maintaining the ICT facilities.

The colleges use only a small proportion of their budget to develop ICT provision. About half the colleges have identified financial priorities to achieve an appropriate balance between meeting the demands for resources of the normal curriculum and developing an effective ICT infrastructure. Only one-third have determined the funding requirements needed to ensure all students have suitable opportunities to benefit from high quality ICT facilities. Only one-quarter of the colleges have sought and received funding from industry for the development of ICT provision. These are mainly large colleges with good industry links.

Approximately 80% of lecturers do not use ICT regularly to support and improve the quality of the students' learning. Most lecturers do not have the competence and confidence to integrate ICT into their teaching strategies. Although the further education sector has invested significantly in developing ICT facilities, they are not used to achieve their full potential in supporting teaching and learning.

The development and use of ICT varies considerably between vocational areas. In engineering, construction and computer studies, ICT is used regularly and effectively by about half of the lecturers. Approximately one-quarter of lecturers in business, science, and in programmes for students with special learning difficulties and disabilities have developed a good level of competence in ICT and have the confidence to plan and use it in their teaching strategies. Less than one-tenth of lecturers in art and design, health and social care, leisure and tourism and basic skills programmes plan and use ICT in their teaching strategies.

There is almost no use of ICT by lecturers on GCSE and GCE A level courses. Only a small number of the colleges assess the ICT skills of all new students to identify the level of support required to help them use the ICT resources effectively. Almost all colleges provide full-time students on vocational courses with an induction programme of basic ICT skills consisting of either timetabled classes or support in open learning centres. The quality of this support is usually good. Approximately half of the colleges are using ICT to improve access to further education and widen participation. In about half of the colleges, the open access centres are well organised and utilised effectively by students from all vocational areas.

A further one-quarter of the colleges have made a good start towards using the open access centres to achieve their full potential to support the students' learning. In the remaining colleges, the centres are poorly organised and not well utilised by students. All the colleges have provided staff development programmes in ICT. Although about two-thirds of lecturers have had basic training in ICT, most do not have the competence and confidence to integrate it into their teaching strategies. About half of the colleges have carried out an assessment of lecturers' expertise in using ICT. Only one-quarter, however, have used the results to identify clearly programme areas where there are skills shortages. Few of the colleges have an effective staff development programme to ensure there are sufficient well-qualified technicians.

There is a general shortage of high-quality interactive learning materials across all curriculum areas. In all of the colleges, only a few lecturers have participated in curriculum development initiatives in ICT.

The further education sector has been the focus of a number of important Government initiatives aimed at promoting the effective use of ICT to support teaching and learning. In 1996, the Learning and Technology Committee of the Further Education Funding Council (FEFC) chaired by Sir Gordon Higginson made a number of recommendations for meeting the ICT needs of the FE sector in Great Britain. Since 1996, the then Department of Education for Northern Ireland (DENI) established a number of working groups and published their respective strategy documents to take forward the recommendations of the Higginson report.

DENI has subsequently approved priorities for action for the development of ICT in the further education sector and advised that the development of the National Grid for Learning (NGfL) and the University for Industry (UfI) should underpin their implementation and promote the concept of lifelong learning. The Strategy Group on Education Technology was established by DENI in April 1996 to advise on the strategy to be pursued for the development and application of education technology in schools, teacher education and further education; to maintain and update the strategy in light of developments; and to advise DENI on the action plan required to give effect to the strategy. The strategy was published in October 1997 and recommended for the further education sector:

—a competence-based model of education technology certification for teachers;

—a programme of in-service training; n the provision of networking facilities, including the Internet.

A Strategic Management Group consisting of senior personnel representatives from DENI, Curriculum Advisory and Support Services, school and library authorities was formed to implement the strategy in a coherent and collaborative way. It has responsibility for putting in place the Northern Ireland components of the NGfL and of the major programme of ICT training for teachers to be financed by the New Opportunities Fund. The strategy focuses mainly on schools but has a general application to the further education sector. In September 1997, DENI established the Education and Learning Technologies Working Group. Its remit was to take account of:

— the current use of technology in the further education sector in Northern Ireland;

— the potential impact of new developments in technology, on the teaching and learning process within further education colleges in Northern Ireland;

— the emerging curriculum framework that will inform future developments in the further education sector; in the effectiveness of the use of the new technology in colleges and the benefit to the learners; and to recommend:

  — ways of increasing the use of educational technology to improve the provision of further education, including the effectiveness of students' learning;

  — methods of disseminating information on good practice in the application of new technology;

  — the resource implications of recommendations.

In 1998, the Education and Learning Technology Working Group recommended that the Department should:

— devise and implement a sector-wide policy and strategy for the integration of an integrated ICT network for the further and higher education sector;

— connect all colleges to an ICT network infrastructure;

— provide a coherent curriculum and staff development programme for the effective implementation of ICT by all staff;

— establish appropriate management information systems.

DENI established subsequently the Further Education Information and Communications Strategy Group to identify key priority areas for action to ensure the successful implementation of these recommendations. The Strategy Group proposed the following priority areas for action:

— the development of college policies and strategies for ICT;

—staff development to ensure all staff can competently use ICT;

— the development of curriculum materials;

— increasing student access to ICT facilities;

— the establishment of appropriate management information systems;

— the development of appropriate ICT infrastructures based on common standards and protocols.

In June 1999, DENI approved the priorities for action proposed by the Further Education Information and Communications Strategy Group and advised that the objectives of the Government's policy on Lifelong Learning should underpin their implementation. The priorities for action for the further education sector over the next three years are to:

— develop compatible internal infrastructures which allow ICT to be exploited to its full potential;

— create a regional area network to connect further education colleges and higher education institutions;

— establish a staff development programme in the use of ICT, based on an agreed specification and existing qualifications;

— deliver the staff development programme agreed by colleges in an effective and efficient way;

— ensure all full-time lecturers are trained by 2002/3 and to commence training part-time lecturers after this date;

— promote curriculum development among lecturers to ensure the development of suitable ICT learning materials.

The Government recognises also that the development of the NGfL and the UfI should facilitate the concept of Lifelong Learning through using ICT to its maximum potential. The Government's strategic aim of developing a new culture of Lifelong Learning throughout Northern Ireland presents a major challenge to the further education sector which is the main provider of vocational education and training for young people and adults. Recent evidence shows that 40% of the unemployed and 19% of the employed in Northern Ireland have no qualifications, and 58% of the employed population do not have a level 3 qualification. In addition, a Gallup Poll in 1996 indicated that only 28% of the population in Northern Ireland had recently engaged in formal learning compared to 40% in England.

Lifelong Learning has a major contribution to make towards providing those who are in employment and those looking for work with up-to-date skills and knowledge. As a result, new demands have been placed on colleges of further education to increase provision and to widen access to education and training. This will require greater flexibility in recruitment and new approaches to teaching and learning including the development and use of ICT. To contribute towards the achievement of the objectives of Lifelong Learning, colleges of further education are required to expand significantly and improve learning opportunities for all sections of the community.

The objectives of the Lifelong Learning strategy have implications for the development of ICT. They are to:

— increase significantly adult participation in vocational education and training, including access to further and higher education and training from groups previously under-represented;

— emphasise the development of basic and key skills;

— ensure greater ease of progression through the system of qualifications;

— provide a more coherent relationship between education and training provision and the skills needed for the regional economy;

— enhance collaboration between education and training providers and the world of business and industry;

— enhance significantly the information and communication skills of teachers, instructors and students;

— sustain and improve the quality of provision and enhance the performance across the education and training sectors.

The Government has drawn up an action plan for the next three years to ensure the objectives of the Lifelong Learning strategy are achieved and a new culture of lifelong learning is established. A number of targets set by the action plan have major implications for the further education sector. These include:

— launching the UfI in 2000 to promote and market education and training;

— developing more flexible modes of provision so as to facilitate increased participation in learning;

— introducing a Strategic Collaboration Fund in 1999 to enhance partnership in adult education;

— education and training between further education colleges and the main stakeholders;

— expanding significantly participation in further education by 8,000 full-time and part-time places by 2002.

Central to the success of the strategy for Lifelong Learning is the UfI which will build on the NGfL. These initiatives will exploit modern information and communication technologies, including the Internet and CD-ROMs, to make learning more flexible, available and cost-effective. By the year 2000, the UfI will be launched nationally and will develop close links with private organisations, colleges of further education and schools. The targets for the NGfL by 2002 include connecting all schools, colleges, universities and public libraries to the NGfL, and ensuring that serving lecturers feel confident and are competent to teach using ICT within the curriculum. A Northern Ireland Network for Education (NINE) has been established as the local node for NGfL and the further education sector has a major role to play in its development.

The results was indicate that about four-fifths of lecturers in the further education sector do not use ICT regularly to support and improve the quality of the students' learning. Despite having had basic training in ICT, most lecturers do not have the competence and confidence to integrate ICT into their teaching strategies. Although the further education sector has invested significantly in developing ICT facilities including computer systems, networks and open access centres, they are not used to achieve their full potential in supporting teaching and learning.

The development and use of ICT in teaching and learning varies considerably between programme areas. In computer studies, construction and engineering, ICT is used regularly and effectively by about half of lecturers. Approximately one-quarter of lecturers in business, science, and in programmes for students with special learning difficulties and disabilities have developed a good level of competence in ICT and have the confidence to plan and use it in their teaching strategies. Less than one-tenth of lecturers in art and design, health and social care, leisure and tourism and basic skills programmes plan their work to provide students with the opportunity to learn through ICT related tasks. There is almost no use of ICT by lecturers on GCSE and GCE A level courses.

In all colleges, there are enthusiastic staff committed to using ICT to enhance students' learning. They are aware of the many initiatives to develop educational technology and have made a good start to use existing ICT resources to plan and support teaching in a range of programme areas. Most staff are not aware, however, of the potential of ICT to support and improve teaching and learning. They lack confidence in using new technology and have not been provided with suitable opportunities to develop competence in ICT and to integrate it into their teaching methods. In some programme areas, committed staff are not able to use ICT effectively because of insufficient or outdated computer systems and ICT infrastructures or a limited range of software. They are also hindered by the lack of, or inadequate implementation of strategies for ICT development.

Approximately half the colleges are implementing suitable policies and strategies for the development of ICT and are benefiting from their investments. Staff are starting to integrate ICT successfully into teaching and learning methods and the colleges are investigating new approaches to use ICT to increase participation rates in education. Only a small number of colleges assess the ICT skills of all new students to identify the level of support required to help them use the ICT resources effectively. In the other colleges, the initial assessment of students' ICT skills is left to the discretion of individual programme co-ordinators.

All colleges enrol students with a wide range of competences in ICT. Many have excellent skills in ICT, however, a significant number progress from school to full-time and part-time courses with poor ICT skills and are unable to cope sufficiently with the demands of their courses. For example, in a full-time technician course in construction, approximately half of the students had no previous experience of ICT and could not engage in a simple computer-assisted-drafting exercise. The lecturer was given no information about the students' level of competence in ICT and was unable to provide appropriate support during the lesson.

Almost all colleges provide full-time students on vocational courses with an induction programme of basic ICT skills consisting of either timetabled classes or support in open learning centres. The quality of this support is usually good. Students acquire basic competences and are able to word-process, create spreadsheets and interrogate databases although few are accredited with a qualification. Most full-time students on academic courses are not provided with planned opportunities to learn relevant ICT skills. Students enrolled on part-time vocational courses are seldom provided with induction programmes and they develop their ICT skills only when it is needed as part of their course.

The provision for part-time students wishing to address significant weaknesses in ICT is generally inadequate. Only a minority are provided with good guidance on relevant courses and open access facilities to achieve accreditation in basic ICT skills. In most colleges, students with learning difficulties and/or disabilities have good access to ICT facilities. They are provided with up to three hours each week to develop a wide range of experiences in ICT including word-processing, CD-ROMs, Internet and the use of electronic mail (E-mail).

Approximately half the colleges are using ICT to improve access to further education and widen participation. One effective strategy is to transport high specification laptop computer systems to community and outreach centres to deliver a range of part-time courses in IT. This provision has increased significantly the participation of adult community groups in further education. Most of the adults enrolled on the courses have had little or no previous experience of further education and lack confidence in their ability to learn.

The courses are well planned and prepared and provide the students with challenging learning experiences. The students are encouraged to learn independently and are motivated to achieve qualifications in IT. Another innovative strategy for widening participation is the Adapt programme where a college is piloting a new computer-based learning system. This allows students from a distant location using high specification, on-line computer facilities to connect to a central CD-ROM server based in the college and provides access to a wide range of training programmes customised to meet individual requirements.

Small to medium enterprises in agriculture, retail and tourism involving 120 managers ranging in age from 30 to 70 have been selected for the pilot. Most of these students have not participated previously in further education and have little experience of ICT. The aim of the programme is to accelerate the acquisition of new ICT skills and to increase the competitiveness of industry. The above strategies indicate that widening participation to further education is best achieved by increasing the flexibility of the ICT facilities available to students and providing them with good access to relevant information and well designed learning materials.

In about half the colleges open access centres with up-to-date computer systems are well organised and utilised by students from all vocational areas. They are encouraging students to take greater responsibility for their own learning and to work independently. A further one-quarter of colleges have made a good start towards using the open access centres to achieve their full potential to support the students' learning. In the remaining colleges, the centres are poorly organised and not well utilised by students. Staff in these centres are not clear on their roles and responsibilities and do not provide students with suitable guidance and support. In addition, there is limited good quality software and other resources. As a result, students are not motivated and do not utilise fully the computer systems. The main use by students of the computer systems in open access centres is limited to word-processing assignments and creating spreadsheets.

The use of databases is confined mainly to technology-based and business-related curriculum areas. Students benefit most from open access centres when they engage in challenging computer-based tasks set by their vocational tutors and have developed the necessary ICT skills to make full use of the computer systems. Although all colleges are connected to the Internet, most have few connection points and provide limited access for students. In addition, few staff have incorporated the application of the Internet into their teaching methods.

As a result, the Internet is not well used to support students' learning. A minority of students use it to obtain information or data on specialist areas for their assignment work. Most, however, do not have sufficient skills to use it competently and spend too much time collecting unnecessary information. In colleges with open access arrangements to the Internet, staff are encouraged to integrate its use into their teaching methods and to provide the students with suitable support in developing their expertise to use it effectively. Students on higher education courses in four colleges benefit significantly from using the Joint Academic Network (JANET) to communicate with local universities and use a range of information sources including video conferencing.

In all colleges, there is wide use of video recordings in vocational and most academic courses. In the best practice, the use of video recordings is planned and integrated effectively into the students' learning. Students benefit from observing well-documented relevant experiences recorded on video and use them to discuss and apply them to their work. Frequently, however, the video is watched out of context by students who are unable to understand its relevance to their subject area. Many video recordings used in teaching are outdated. Audio tapes are used effectively in all colleges, mainly in courses in modern languages and media studies. In a few colleges, high quality specialist computer-based audio facilities are used to teach music courses. They provide students with excellent experiences in working with electronic-based music.

There is practically no planned use of ICT to support teaching and learning in GCSE and GCE A level courses. The majority of lecturers in academic studies have not acquired a basic level of competence in the use of ICT. In English, geography, history and mathematics, there are almost no computer-based learning materials available for students, even in colleges with well organised open access centres and good ICT facilities. Two colleges provide a limited range of CD-ROMs and software application packages in mathematics for students to learn independently. A small number of students use ICT to present their work using word-processing, particularly in English. Exceptionally, one or two students use the Internet to retrieve information for use in their assignments. They obtain authentic material on a wide range of specific topics which considerably broadens their vocabulary.

In most colleges, good use is made of video and audio equipment on GCSE and GCE A level courses in modern languages for students to present, practise and consolidate their language skills. Satellite television and video conferencing are used by students in two colleges to communicate with language students in other countries. These students have excellent learning experiences and gain a good understanding of the cultures associated with the language development. One college has commissioned a new computer-based language laboratory which has the facility to link to the Internet. Students have good opportunities to work independently and co-operate well with other students in group projects.

The use of the laboratory is not yet exploited to its full potential. There is a considerable variation in the competence of lecturers of modern languages to integrate ICT into their teaching strategies. In two colleges, all lecturers have had effective staff development on the use of the Internet and confidently create appropriate websites. The majority of lecturers do not, however, use ICT sufficiently to enhance the students' learning.

The planned use of ICT in teaching and learning is limited in art and design to those lecturers with specific interest in ICT and, there is significant variation in the degree to which the staff are able to use ICT in teaching and learning. The level of competence of many lecturers is limited to the use of word-processing, databases and spreadsheets and the majority have not progressed to using the broader applications of ICT, for example, CD-ROMs in a formal teaching situation. In contrast, considerable use is made of CD-ROMs by art and design students, for example, in the research of progression opportunities in employment and higher education and in the research of historical and contemporary art and design. Many students use ICT to produce graphics but it is rarely used for three-dimensional, textiles and fashion or interior and spacial design.

Many colleges have retained a small number of Apple Macintosh machines solely for art and design purposes but they are usually out of date and poorly maintained. The quality and quantity of hardware installed with specialist art and design software is, in the majority of cases, poor. In a few instances there are small numbers of up-to-date machines with appropriate software; these are heavily used and, as a result, are frequently out of order. While the use of digital cameras has been introduced successfully in a small number of colleges there are large numbers of students wishing to access a single camera.

The use and development of ICT in teaching and learning in art and design are underdeveloped and the quality and standards of specialist software and hardware are inadequate. The opportunities for staff to undertake staff development on a subject basis are insufficient.

Basic Skills

The provision of basic skills for students on basic skills programmes is generally poor. The use of ICT in basic skills is largely limited to old and slow machines running dated and limited software packages. Lecturers, however, do manage to maximise the potential of these facilities and many students succeed in developing a basic range of keyboarding skills in word-processing and drafting letters. In one college the students on basic skills programmes use very simple software packages to develop their number skills and improve their understanding of measurement, height, weight and time.

Problems with hardware and its incompatibility with main college ICT facilities cause problems in many colleges which often result in students being unfamiliar with the different operating systems and unable to use the ICT facilities in the main college library or open learning centre. In only one college are interactive learning programmes in basic skills used to good effect. The IT skills of the majority of students are poor. The work is highly prescriptive and most of the students require regular direction and intervention from their tutors. In many cases the students are not proficient at accessing software, files and databases or in saving and printing their own work.

The level of investment in ICT for basic skill classes is poor. In many colleges the classes are located in cramped and damp mobiles and are allocated the oldest computers and printers, some of which are almost obsolete. In one college the recent purchase of new computers has not been matched with the supply of appropriate software, however, funds have been allocated to rectify this in the coming year. In around half of the colleges the move towards mainly personal computer (PC) hardware has disadvantaged many of the students in basic skills who are still taught mainly on older systems. In basic skills the use of ICT is not well developed and students are disadvantaged by the allocation of old machines no longer required by other departments and courses.

All colleges need to invest in the specialist hardware and software for basic skills work and in doing so to ensure that the operating systems are compatible with the college's open access ICT facilities.

In the majority of classes where ICT is used by vocational lecturers, the quality of teaching and learning is good. In one college, for example, a lecturer has trained students to use the Internet to research the social and economic profiles of countries and to evaluate export marketing opportunities. The key skill classes in IT are well planned and provide students with good opportunities to develop competence across all the elements of the key skill. In most colleges, the IT lecturers collaborate with the vocational specialists to integrate the teaching of the key skill in an appropriate vocational context. Students have good opportunities, for example, to integrate their knowledge of spreadsheet techniques with cash flow forecasts.

The use of ICT, however, in assignment briefs is underdeveloped in the majority of colleges and the students have insufficient opportunities to develop and reinforce the skills learned in the IT classes. Most of the students have satisfactory or better IT skills, especially in word-processing, spreadsheets and databases. A significant minority of students have poor skills in researching, interpreting and disseminating information from the Internet.

In the majority of colleges, the computer rooms are utilised fully for IT key skills classes and most of the computers are stand-alone and dated. In one college, a lecturer who was using an interactive accounting learning package with a Higher National Certificate class did not have access to a networked computer room. A considerable amount of time was wasted installing seven floppy disks on each computer before the class could begin. Most lecturers in business have developed good skills in IT and a significant minority of them use their own personal computers at home to produce teaching resources. However, most are not confident in the use of ICT in the classroom and their knowledge of the resources which are available is poor.

There is insufficient use of ICT in teaching and learning in business and staff require more support in the use of ICT as a teaching tool. In addition, there is insufficient access to networked computer rooms for nearly all business courses. Students have good opportunities to develop their IT skills when they are integrated effectively into the assignment programme.

Computing

Although almost all of the lecturers in the vocational area of computing have high levels of expertise in ICT, there is considerable variation in the use of educational technology to improve and enhance the quality of teaching and learning. In most colleges the computing courses are well organised and provide students with good opportunities to develop practical ICT skills in vocationally relevant applications. However, little use is made of computer-based learning techniques. A small number of lecturers make good use of data projection equipment for software and other demonstrations but most lecturers make insufficient use of presentation software in the delivery of lessons and there are few examples of the use of CD-ROM materials, multimedia packages, video conferencing or the Internet to support learning. In a minority of colleges, the students make good use of the Internet to access technical support sites when designing and developing computer programs. In the majority of colleges, the integration and use of the Internet as a teaching strategy is underdeveloped; student access is often limited and expensive.

In about half of the colleges, the resources used to deliver computing do not meet modern standards. In these colleges many of the computers are unable to run some of the more advanced software tools and the students have insufficient opportunity to use up-to-date computer systems. This inhibits the use of educational technology by lecturers to develop the students' use of relational databases, presentation software and the design of computer programs in programming languages which involve object orientated and event-driven programming. In one-third of colleges, the networks provide students with access to good on-line learning materials where they work independently to develop ICT skills in a variety of industry-standard application packages. In these colleges, lecturers integrate educational technology effectively into their teaching strategies and the students' learning in computing is enhanced. In computing, while the ICT skills of lecturers are well-developed, there is little integration of ICT into their teaching and learning strategies.

All of the colleges provide good opportunities for students on technician programmes at level 3 and above to develop a range of ICT skills. In contrast, the use of ICT on craft programmes at levels 2 and 3 is not well developed. The main provision at level 3 is the inclusion of work using computer-aided draughting packages for the design and architectural detailing of a variety of construction projects. The colleges provide opportunities for students to take the City and Guilds (C&G) 4351 programme in addition to the BTEC national diploma or advanced GNVQ programmes which they take as their main studies. Opportunities are also provided for students to use word-processing packages and spreadsheets.

The quality of teaching and learning in the use of computer-aided draughting is at different stages of development. In about half of the programmes the work is well developed. The students have very good learning experiences and the quality of their work is excellent. In about one-quarter of the programmes the use of computer-aided draughting is satisfactory and continues to develop. The students have acquired the basic concepts but still need to develop their expertise in the use of specialist architectural packages. In about one-quarter of the programmes the use of computer-aided draughting is at an early stage of development in terms of access to modern hardware, software and developing the skills in a vocational context. However, now that access to the equipment and software is improving these weaknesses should be addressed.

Good use is made of ICT in the teaching of environmental science. Most of the students use spreadsheets for tabulated calculations such as heat loss from buildings and most use word-processors for their assignments. Presentation software is not used extensively. In contrast, the students use Powerpoint for presenting aspects of their projects and use data-logging software for surveying. The quality of the work produced by the students is to the standard required for the C&G 4351. Where they have opportunities to use architectural packages, the quality of the students' work is excellent and is displayed effectively. The display of this work is useful to promote high standards and provides prospective students with insights into the nature and quality of the work undertaken on the construction programmes.

The accommodation and equipment for ICT in about half of the construction programmes are good. The hardware is modern and is located in rooms refurbished with the specialist furnishings. About one-quarter have an inappropriate mix of modern and out-dated equipment. There is modern hardware and software in about one-quarter of the programmes but the computers have yet to be linked to an effective network. In construction, the use of ICT is strongest in technician programmes and in the use of software for computer-aided draughting. It is weakest in craft programmes at level 2 and 3.

The main areas for development are in the expansion of the work in material science in environmental science and in surveying. More use needs to be made of ICT as a teaching tool by staff and as a presentation tool by students.

Engineering

In engineering, the design of all GNVQ and BTEC diploma or certificate courses, which are offered by colleges at levels 2, 3 and 4 to technician students, incorporate specialist units of study which require students to use and apply a suitable range of specialist and generic IT skills. These technician courses are provided for full-time students and, as additional studies, for part-time technician and craft students, most of whom are modern apprentices working towards an NVQ at level 3. This high quality IT provision contrasts with the provision in many of the NVQ and C&G craft courses at levels 2 and 3 which offer the development of a narrow range of IT skills or no specialist IT skills at all. The introduction of the key skill of IT as a requirement in all modern apprenticeships should ensure that all future craft students develop a broad range of generic IT skills even if they choose not to take any additional studies.

The standard of teaching of specialist IT in engineering is never less than satisfactory and is generally good. The majority of the lecturers have worked hard to keep themselves up-to-date with modern engineering technologies and to ensure that students are challenged by well planned lectures, prograammes and relevant assignments. The quality of the physical resources for use by engineering students has improved dramatically in most colleges during the last three years and, within each college, this normally sets the limit of the match between the experiences which the students receive and the needs of modern industry. For example, across the colleges, technician students consistently have good or better opportunities to develop their abilities in computer-aided design in mechanical and electrical engineering whereas their experiences in modern computer-aided manufacture, the control of mechanical and electrical power systems, and computer-assisted learning in electronics are good or excellent in only around one-half of the colleges.

Apart from the development of the specialist IT skills of the students, less than one-third of the lecturers use IT widely as a means to enhance the learning experiences of the students. In general, the use of the Internet and commercially produced CD-ROMs and computer-assisted learning software is underdeveloped. Two excellent examples were observed where the lecturers had developed their own high quality computer-assisted learning software; one lecturer used software effectively to integrate the teaching of engineering science and mathematics to improve the understanding of the students and another lecturer used distance learning material to teach computer-aided design on a course which attracted employees from industry with a wide range of prior experience of computer-aided design.

Technician students demonstrate a satisfactory or good standard of specialist ICT skills, particularly in the computer-aided design of mechanical components and of electronic circuits and systems. In general, they display good standards in the key skill of IT. This contrasts with craft students, the majority of whom do not develop competence in a broad range of IT skills. Few engineering students use the Internet to search out information for themselves. In general, the provision for technician students in engineering to develop their specialist IT skills and their key skills of IT is good and the standards achieved by the students are never less than satisfactory and mostly good or excellent. The provision for craft students is not designed to ensure that all of them have opportunities to develop a wide range of either specialist IT skills or the key skill of IT.

The provision of ICT in health and social care ranges from satisfactory to poor but is mostly poor. In the satisfactory provision, the students have timetabled classes in IT and have access to open learning centres to use computers to word-process assignments, CD-ROMs for information, and the Internet for access to relevant databases such as the Child Care Web Page. In the poor provision, there is little available beyond of the timetabled provision for the key skill of IT.

The use of ICT in teaching and learning in health and social care is generally poor; only around 25% is good. The majority of the specialist teachers have little experience in ICT and are unaware of the resources available to support their teaching. The students have a good understanding of IT because of the key skill of IT and, from their assignments, can undertake competently word-processing, spreadsheets and data presentation. They are less competent in using CD-ROMs and the Internet to access information and databases to support their assignments and projects. The assignment programmes generally have no specific requirements for the students to access CD-ROMs or the Internet. This is due mainly to the teachers' lack of knowledge of what is available and how its use could be integrated into assignments.

The ICT hardware and software resources which are used in health and social care are part of the general college provision. College libraries and/or open learning centres generally provide information on the CD-ROMs available for the use of students and staff; often, the information provides brief details of what is included on each CD-ROM. Access to college Internet facilities is expensive for the students.

The use of ICT in teaching and learning in health and social care is generally poor. Whilst all specialist teachers have participated in basic ICT training, this has only been developed further in health and social care in a minority of colleges. Further training is required to strengthen the ICT knowledge and expertise of the majority of specialist teachers in health and social care and its application and use in teaching and learning.

Tourism Students

The main ICT provision for leisure and tourism students is an average of one taught hour per week in the key skill of IT. In most cases, the vocational lecturers meet with the specialist IT lecturers to identify together appropriate opportunities to develop the key skill through vocational and occupational units of study. ICT is used confidently by less than 10% of leisure and tourism lecturers to improve teaching and learning. In the best examples, the students are required to use the Internet or CD-ROMs to seek and assess information for assignments.

The links developed between the vocational tutors and the key skill specialists provide limited opportunities to develop IT skills in vocationally relevant contexts. For example, in a GNVQ advanced course the survey data collected by the students for use in a marketing unit was analysed and annotated by students in the IT class using spreadsheets and presentational software. In one college, however, none of the advanced leisure and tourism students had accessed the Internet. In all colleges the students are encouraged to word-process their assignments and in one college the students on GNVQ advanced course and students on NVQ travel services courses are trained in the use of a computerised holiday reservation system. This specialised software training package enables the students to practice specific IT skills in a simulated situation before entering the workplace. In contrast in another college, the attendance of students at key skill classes is poor and consequently their progress is poor.

Access to ICT facilities in well resourced classrooms and learning resource centres is good in 50% of the colleges. In one college there has been significant investment specifically for leisure and tourism courses. There is a suite of networked multimedia PCs with dedicated technical support. Despite being at an early stage of development, particularly in the purchase of appropriate software for the vocational area, significant steps have been taken to improve the opportunities to integrate ICT into aspects of the leisure and tourism curriculum. The lack of an adequate network infrastructure, however, and generally low level of ICT resources in the remainder of the colleges hinder student access to important sources of ICT based information.

The level of ICT knowledge and expertise varies amongst full-time and part-time staff across the vocational area. In 75% of the colleges the awareness of staff of current ICT developments has been raised through the attendance at staff development courses in the Oxford and Cambridge RSA Computer Literacy and Information Technology (CLAIT) courses and a series of short courses in the use of CD-ROMs, the Internet and Powerpoint. In one college, a specialist IT lecturer has been seconded to assist in the design and delivery of ICT training for all college staff and the lecturers are encouraged to follow a Joint Examining Board certificate in the educational use of IT. Despite these staff development initiatives across the colleges, only a small number of lecturers in leisure and tourism use ICT effectively in their teaching and learning.

Science

Approximately half of the colleges make good use of ICT as a learning and teaching resource for science. These colleges place a strong emphasis on the use of ICT to develop the science curriculum and tools such as proprietary software, data-logging equipment and the Internet and intranet materials are used well to enhance and enrich the students' learning experiences. In contrast, in the other colleges little use is made of ICT in science classes. In the best practice, the science lecturers give considerable thought and attention to selecting aspects of the curriculum which can be enhanced by the use of ICT. In one college, for example, the use of a microscope, a flexi-camera and a visual display unit has helped the advanced GNVQ students to gain a good understanding of aspects of histology. In another large college the lecturers have developed Internet and intranet materials which are customised for use by the students. A useful booklet on methods of accessing the Internet provide the students with excellent guidance on finding and using information and contributes significantly to the development of the students' information handling skills.

There is a general shortage of resources for ICT for both staff and students. While many colleges have used funding from the Further Education Programme to enhance and expand software and hardware, generally the staff and students do not have sufficient access to modern equipment and resources. Although many students have access to IT facilities outside normal timetabled classes, they have insufficient access to specialist software. The use of ICT as a teaching and learning resource for science is beginning to be developed in colleges. The quality of the provision varies widely. Well focused staff development is required to raise the profile of ICT as a

Provision for students with learning difficulties and disabilities includes programmes for people with physical disabilities, as well as provision for individuals with mild, moderate or severe learning difficulties. The provision for students with physical disabilities is generally good. Many colleges provide special aids and adaptations which promote inclusive learning for students with physical disabilities. Examples of such aids in use in colleges are the special guard which enables one student with cystic fibrosis to use a computer and the sound facility which provides computer access for blind students. The provision for students with learning difficulties and disabilities is more variable. In the provision which is good in approximately 20% of the colleges, the students have regular access to computers and good quality software packages. Poor provision is characterised by equipment which is outdated and a lack of staff awareness that ICT can be used to support learning for these students.

The use of ICT in teaching and learning for students with learning difficulties and disabilities is generally satisfactory. In the best practice, CD-ROMs are used to support teaching in areas such as basic first aid, and students benefit from using desktop publishing applications in, for example, designing Christmas cards as part of a mini-enterprise programme. In a number of colleges in which specialist staff have developed expertise in the use of ICT, customised computer packages are used to help students with moderate learning difficulties to improve their literacy and numeracy skills. On the other hand, some of the specialist teachers have little experience in ICT and only a limited understanding of the resources available to support teaching and learning.

Students' abilities to use ICT are related directly to the quality of the equipment available, the access which they have to appropriate packages which are relevant and age-appropriate, and the expertise in ICT of the staff supporting these programmes. Many of the lecturers require additional training if they are to realise the potential of the use of ICT with these students. At times, standards are affected adversely as a consequence of insufficient co-ordination between the specialist lecturers and those who are teaching basic skills. In one college, this is leading to insufficient progression in the development of the students' skills in the use of ICT. The quality of ICT hardware and software resources which is used for students with learning difficulties and disabilities is good in approximately 20% of the colleges. In the remaining colleges the only equipment available to students is outdated and, at times, almost obsolete. There is considerable variation in staff awareness of the software packages which are suitable for students with moderate and severe learning difficulties.

One of the problems in this area is the identification of computer packages which take direct account of the needs of young people and adults; many of the packages are designed for children of primary school age and have little to offer older students. Staff awareness of the ways in which ICT can be used to support teaching and learning for students with learning difficulties and disabilities is increasing but there remains a need for staff training and development which focuses on the identification and application of specialist equipment for use with these students.

In a minority of colleges, the only equipment which is available to the students on a regular basis is outdated. There is a need to upgrade the facilities available for these students and to extend the use of selected software packages to improve the learning of students.

In recent years, all colleges have provided staff development programmes in ICT. To date, about two-thirds of lecturers have acquired a basic level of competence in ICT and a minority have progressed to higher qualifications. In most colleges, a minority of staff from a wide range of vocational areas have benefited from well-organised specialist courses and have achieved high levels of competence in ICT. A few colleges have included technicians in the staff development programmes for ICT training. Most of the staff development programmes have been delivered in colleges by lecturers with suitable expertise though a few have been provided by outside organisations.

About half the colleges have carried out an assessment of lecturers' expertise in ICT, usually through a questionnaire. Only one-quarter of colleges have used, however, the results of the assessment to identify clearly areas where there are skills shortages in ICT and to design programmes to meet the specific curricular needs of lecturers. The staff development programmes provide training mainly in word-processing, spreadsheets, databases, and the use of CD-ROMs and the Internet, but do not focus sufficiently on the use of ICT to support teaching and learning.

Few colleges have an effective staff development programme to ensure there are sufficient well-qualified technicians for ICT work. A number of colleges have recruited technicians with high levels of expertise who are able to maintain and commission computer systems, networks, video conferencing equipment and satellite facilities. They work competently with lecturers and students during lessons to ensure all systems are functional. In the majority of colleges, the technicians have been in long-term employment and have little expertise in the maintenance and commissioning of ICT systems and require significant levels of retraining. Frequently in these colleges, ICT equipment which has failed remains out of service for long periods of time.

About half the colleges have established appropriate procedures for the review and evaluation of the effectiveness of the staff development programmes in ICT. Although weaknesses have been identified, suitable action is not always taken to ensure the staff development programmes led to an improvement in the quality of the teaching and learning.

Curriculum Development

Colleges recognise that there is a general shortage of good quality interactive learning materials across all curriculum areas which are suitable for students with a wide range of ability and interests. Approximately one-quarter of colleges have acquired a satisfactory range of commercially-produced interactive learning materials. Lecturers with expertise in ICT have identified and purchased suitable CD-ROMs and specialist software applications which meet specific needs in a range of curriculum areas and promote the use of ICT in teaching and learning. For example, CD-ROMS are used in health and social care to access relevant information, Autocad software packages are used for students to learn draughting skills, students in travel courses use software for travel accommodation and reservations and accounting software is used for business applications.

These packages cater for a wide range of interests and abilities and allow students to work on their own. The remaining colleges provide students with only a limited range of interactive learning materials which significantly inhibits the effective use of the ICT facilities for teaching and learning. In almost all colleges, there is little use of interactive learning materials to deliver programmes in basic skills. In all colleges, there are only small numbers of lecturers who have benefited from curriculum development initiatives in ICT.

Most lecturers do not have sufficient expertise to evaluate or produce relevant and challenging interactive learning materials which allow students to work independently. In recent years, a limited range of ICT curricular materials have been produced by colleges working independently or in consortia. The Telematics curriculum development initiative funded through DENI Further Education Programme, involved staff from a number of colleges who produced interactive learning materials for four vocational areas; construction and the built environment, health and social care, hospitality and catering, and science. A CD-ROM was produced containing material for use on NVQ, GNVQ and GCE A level courses.

The quality of the interactive learning materials is good and has been disseminated to all colleges. In a large college, the lecturers on adult basic education programmes produced a specialist software package for the computer-based assessment of basic skills. Lecturers who have participated in curriculum development initiatives have developed a high-level of awareness of the application of ICT to support teaching and learning.

Approximately half the colleges have devised appropriate written policies and strategies for the development and use of ICT across the curriculum. They are comprehensive and reflect recent Government initiatives aimed at promoting the effective use of educational technology and the concept of Lifelong Learning. The policies and strategies are wide-ranging and identify important implications for:

— college management; n curriculum and staff development;

— access arrangements for students;

— the standardisation of ICT hardware and software resources;

— technical support;

— support for students with learning difficulties and/or disabilities;

— the monitoring and evaluation of the effectiveness of ICT in supporting students' learning.

The policies and strategies have been prepared by at least one senior manager with expertise in ICT working closely with the principal or director and other senior staff, normally through a committee established for the development of ICT across the college. Realistic targets and time scales have been set for their implementation and the roles and responsibilities of staff are clearly defined. The ICT policies and strategies are included in the CDP and are approved by the governing body. The development of suitable policies and strategies for ICT is at an early stage in about one-fifth of colleges. Although senior management teams are setting realistic targets for the development of an ICT infrastructure, insufficient emphasis is placed on the use of ICT to support teaching and learning.

Approximately one-third of colleges have not produced written policies or strategies for the development of ICT across the curriculum. As a result, there is no effective planning to use ICT to support teaching and learning, and the development of existing ICT facilities varies considerably between curriculum areas. In addition, there is no coherent cross-college strategy to improve students access to ICT facilities and to develop suitable learning centres and the IT skills of staff and students. In particular, the needs of students with learning difficulties and/or disabilities are not assessed and met.

The development of ICT in these colleges is not managed well and progress towards the implementation of an effective ICT infrastructure is poor. Priorities for ICT have not been identified and there are no procedures to monitor the progress of the development of ICT systems. About three-quarters of colleges have established procedures, including codes of conduct, to ensure students use the ICT facilities safely and correctly. On occasions, however, there are insufficient ICT facilities to meet the needs of all students and the procedures are difficult to implement, for example, when a number of students in a class are required to share a computer system to complete a learning task and supervision is weak.

In about 25% of the colleges, students do not have clear codes of conduct when using the ICT systems. In these colleges, access is denied to students at certain times because some computer rooms are unsupervised and locked. In all colleges, there are appropriate policies for students to use and access specialist equipment such as video or satellite systems. Specialist equipment is used by students in specific vocational areas and is not normally for general use. These students are usually competent in using specialist equipment relevant to their vocational area and are provided with open access arrangements. All colleges have recognised the need to establish common standards for hardware and software.

About three-quarters have managed to achieve this objective which has avoided duplication of computer systems, improved the efficiency of the technical support and, allowed the demands from individual programme areas to be planned and delivered more effectively. In about one-quarter of the colleges, however, there is poor co-ordination of the ICT systems with the result that different standards of hardware and software are used across the programme areas. This limits the flexibility of the systems for staff and students and makes maintenance policies more difficult to operate.

In about half of colleges, project groups have worked well to identify the roles and responsibilities of staff, curriculum and staff development needs, and the organisational changes needed to manage ICT successfully across all programme areas. About one-quarter of colleges have identified staff with good expertise in ICT and have given them responsibility for developing strategies to integrate ICT into teaching and learning across the college. This approach has helped staff with little expertise in ICT to introduce it into their teaching methods and has encouraged the development of systems to support students working on their own.

The co-ordination and implementation of ICT across the curriculum is most successful in those colleges where there is strong support from senior management. In these colleges, committees for the development and use of ICT in teaching and learning have been established for senior management to work with committed staff.

As a result, they have produced comprehensive written policies and strategies which are used to develop effectively ICT across the college. Heads of schools and course co-ordinators have been consulted and have contributed significantly to the development and implementation of ICT policies and strategies within their respective programme areas. They have clearly identified the strengths and weaknesses of the current ICT provision, and clarified objectives and time scales for the implementation of ICT learning strategies within individual programmes. The committees have used this information from programme managers to outline clearly the colleges' strategic aims in the use of ICT to support teaching and learning.

The quality of the technical support for the maintenance of the ICT facilities varies considerably across and within colleges. About half of the colleges rely mainly on the non-specialist technicians to maintain the computers, together with maintenance contracts agreed with the suppliers when the ICT facilities are acquired. As a result, some ICT equipment is not always maintained in working order. About half the colleges use specialist computer technicians to maintain the ICT systems. This ensures the ICT systems are available for use. There is, however, a significant demand from industry for specialist computer technicians and colleges find it difficult to recruit and retain them. There is a trend for colleges to adopt a policy of leasing ICT facilities to replace outdated systems quickly and cost-effectively, particularly suites of laptop computers for use in outreach centres. Maintenance contracts are included in the leasing arrangements and ensure the ICT facilities are used efficiently.

The senior managers in about half of the colleges have demonstrated a high level of commitment to the development and use of ICT to support teaching and learning. They have devised suitable strategies and policies for the implementation of ICT across the curriculum, and are making good progress towards establishing an effective infrastructure with sufficient high quality computer and communication systems to meet the needs of all students. In addition, the senior managers are investigating ways of using ICT to widen access and increase participation rates in further education. Appropriate procedures for monitoring and evaluating the effectiveness of the policies and strategies have also been established in these colleges. In the remaining colleges, there has been no systematic development of ICT to support teaching and learning. As a result, few lecturers are aware of the potential of ICT to enhance the students' learning.

There are considerable deficiencies in the quality of the ICT facilities across the further education colleges. Only 37% of the computers meet modern requirements and provide comprehensive multimedia facilities and industrial standard software applications. They are used effectively to support teaching and learning by lecturers with good expertise in ICT. Approximately 23% of computers are well over two years old and have limited use; they need to be replaced in the near future. About

40% are about two years old and should be replaced over the next few years. The present ratio of FTEs to computers is 8:1 which is well below the target of 5:1 identified by the further education sector if it is to meet the needs of all students. About one-third of the colleges are making good progress towards establishing advanced network facilities and providing students with good access to multimedia learning materials. Students have open access to the Internet in only four colleges and are beginning to use it to support their learning. There is a need to establish a high bandwidth communications infrastructure linking all colleges to ensure students have access to high-quality multimedia learning materials. Only one-fifth of lecturers use ICT regularly to support and improve teaching and learning, mainly in the vocational areas of engineering, construction and computer studies.

In all colleges the majority of lecturers have been provided with basic training in ICT. Only one-quarter of colleges have, however, identified the extent of the ICT skills shortages in specific programme areas. All colleges need to design and deliver comprehensive and relevant programmes of staff development if lecturers are to have the confidence and competence to integrate ICT into their teaching strategies. The shortage of good quality interactive learning materials inhibits the use of ICT to enhance the students' learning. Few lecturers have engaged in curriculum development projects and have the competence to produce good quality interactive learning materials. Colleges need to ensure that lecturers are able to evaluate and purchase commercially produced interactive learning materials. They also need to work together to develop relevant materials which should be disseminated throughout the further education sector.

Almost all colleges provide students enrolling on full-time vocational courses with an induction programme to develop basic skills in IT. The provision for students with weaknesses in ICT on academic and part-time vocational courses is generally inadequate. In almost all colleges the initial assessment of the ICT skills of new students is poor and lecturers are unable to plan effectively the use of ICT to meet the needs and abilities of all students. As a result, students with poor ICT skills on entry to their programmes struggle significantly during lessons involving the use of ICT. Well managed and equipped open learning centres, including access to the Internet, are encouraging students to work independently in about half the colleges. Lecturers plan their work to ensure students engage in challenging computer-based tasks in the open learning centres.

The organisation and utilisation of the open learning centres is poor in about one-quarter of the colleges. Students are limited to simple word-processing assignments, spend too much time collecting information from the Internet and have insufficient guidance and support from lecturers. To address this issue, senior management needs to ensure that lecturers have a clear understanding of their roles and responsibilities and students use the open learning centres to take greater responsibility for their own learning. Approximately half the colleges have identified and are addressing successfully the factors which influence the development and use of ICT to support and enhance teaching and learning. The remaining colleges need to devise and implement appropriate policies and strategies if ICT is to be integrated effectively into the curriculum.

6

Towards Digitised Education For All

The adoption of 'lifelong education' and 'life-long learning' as guiding principles of educational policy, both in countries that are currently able to provide extensive education and learning opportunities, and in those that are still struggling to eradicate illiteracy and get all children into primary school, represents a commitment to the democratization of education that is limited only by the resources available for its implementation. The impact of this commitment on the development of education beyond the 'elementary and fundamental stages' is the main concern of the present chapter. Enrolments at the secondary and tertiary levels of education taken together account for nearly half of the total enrolment in the world's formal education systems today, compared to barely one-fifth at the time when the Universal Declaration of Human Rights was proclaimed. There are two or three points may be noted in advance.

— Neither 'lifelong education' nor 'lifelong learning', any more so than 'basic education' or 'basic learning needs', are specifically mentioned by the Universal

Declaration of Human Rights or by any of the international treaties relating to education that have been adopted since then. In regard to educational opportunities beyond the 'elementary and fundamental stages', the Declaration proclaims simply that 'Technical and professional education shall be made generally available and higher education shall be equally accessible to all on the basis of merit'. If 'lifelong education' and 'lifelong learning' are nevertheless widely considered to be rooted in the Declaration, it has probably been because the first principle of Article 26, 'Everyone has the right to education', is interpreted to apply throughout life.

— World demographic trends lend support to a 'life-cycle' view of education and learning. The world's population is getting older, thus in principle reducing the burden on the adult population of ensuring the provision of basic education for the younger age groups while at the same time providing scope for increasing educational opportunities at the secondary and tertiary levels, including opportunities at these levels for the continuing education of adults themselves. In the growing number of countries in the more developed regions of the world where a majority of young people today can participate in formal education up until their early twenties, the educational boundaries between youth and adults are dissolving.

— As concerns terminology, 'tertiary education' and 'higher education' are commonly used interchangeably when referring to post-secondary education, unless otherwise indicated. Thus, 'higher education' is understood to have a broader reference than the traditional one of university or equivalent level education. The term 'tertiary education' has come into use internationally with the revised International Standard Classification of Education (ISCED) adopted by the General Conference of UNESCO in 1997.

Although the ideas of 'lifelong education' and 'lifelong learning' have old philosophical roots and can be traced back historically to the earliest efforts to promote universal education, it is unlikely that they would have achieved their current status in educational policies if recent trends and developments in the wider political, economic, social and cultural context had not also been favourable. Both 'lifelong education' and 'lifelong learning' have come to represent in different ways the expectations that societies now have of education and of the scope that should be provided for every individual to develop his or her potential.

Lifelong Education

International interest in the concept of 'lifelong education' was first aroused in the 1960s by discussion and debate within UNESCO concerning the future development of adult education. International co-operation in adult education at that time was complicated by the fact that the challenges facing adult education varied so greatly among countries: in many of the newly independent countries the majority of adults were illiterate, which was not within the recent experience of countries where adult education programmes had long been established. Moreover, among the latter there were many different approaches to adult education. Other than the adult target group itself, there did not exist at that time a unifying principle or concept of adult education that could provide adult educators working in different national circumstances and traditions with a common ideal or purpose, nor one that could settle the question of adult education's status vis-à-vis the regular mainstream education system, to which in most countries adult education was usually regarded as an appendage and very much as a 'poor relation'. Prompted in part by the Second World Conference on Adult Education, which recommended, among other things, that governments should 'regard adult education not as an addition, but as an integral part of their national systems of education', UNESCO's General Conference at its 12th Session two years later took up the matter and went one step further, inviting Member States 'to regard the various forms of out-of-school and adult education as an integral part of any educational system, so that all men and women, throughout their lives, may have the opportunities for pursuing education conducive alike to their individual advancement and to their active participation in civic life and in the social and economic development of their country'.

At the international level, this invitation was the genesis of the idea of 'lifelong education', for it was soon realized, as one of the leading protagonists recalled later, that the design of any coherent overall strategy for the development of out-of-school and adult education would need to consider education as a whole, as well as the succession and interrelation of its various stages over the life-cycle.

The lifelong concept covers all aspects of education, embracing everything in it, with the whole being more than the sum of its parts. There is no such thing as a separate 'permanent' part of education which is not lifelong. In other words, lifelong education is not an educational system but the principle on which the overall organization of a system is founded, and which should accordingly underlie the development of each of its component parts.

Lifelong Learning

By the end of the 1980s, the idea of a 'right to learn' distinct from that of the 'right to education' had gained ground, with the Fourth International Conference on Adult Education, for example, adopting a Declaration on the 'right to learn' that did not actually mention the 'right to education' at all. However, the balance was restored at the Fifth International Conference on Adult Education, with the Conference declaring that 'The recognition of the right to education and the right to learn throughout life is more than ever a necessity'. Since the early 1990s, the trend in educational policies towards a learning-centred view of education generally, and of adult education in particular, has been especially marked in some OECD countries. As far back as the early 1970s, policy-makers in these countries had shared the doubts of the Faure Commission concerning the viability of continued 'linear expansion' of the formal system of full-time education, and in addition were skeptical towards the possibility of further expansion being fully financed by governments. By the end of the 1990s, the idea of public financing of educational opportunities beyond the period of compulsory education had given way in these countries to the idea of shared responsibility or 'partnership' between government, employers and learners themselves.

The kind of education was not anticipated in the Universal Declaration of Human Rights or in any of the international treaties, and States apparently do not feel under an obligation to ensure that such education shall be provided 'free'. In so far as the 'right to lifelong learning' is understood to include a 'right' to continuing education, it would seem in practice to amount to little more than the 'right' of any citizen to participate, at his or her own expense, in the market for goods and services generally, with more or less encouragement from public funds depending on the situation in individual countries. Yet, this was once pretty much the position everywhere in regard to initial education at the secondary and higher levels; it did not last. The readiness of most countries, both rich and poor, to commit public funds for the expansion of educational opportunities beyond the 'elementary and fundamental stages' was to be largely responsible for the worldwide development of secondary and tertiary education that is considered broadly in the sections which follow.

Secondary Education

Secondary education is not actually mentioned in Article 26 of the Universal Declaration of Human Rights. Secondary education at that time was largely oriented towards preparing students for entry to university or equivalent level education. It was probably for these reasons that there was a tendency during the drafting of the Declaration to refer broadly to education above the 'elementary and fundamental stages' as 'higher education'. The first treaty to mention 'secondary education' was the Convention against Discrimination in Education: 'The States Parties [undertake to] make secondary education in its different forms generally available and accessible to all. The International Covenant adopted the same wording, but added the words 'including technical and vocational secondary education' after the word 'forms'. The Convention on the Rights of the Child uses slightly different wording: 'including general and vocational education'.

At first, the expansion was based mainly on existing institutional structures, but in the many countries where there existed different forms of post-elementary education, the type of education to provide soon became an issue. In the 1940s and 1950s, the concept or model of a 'comprehensive' secondary school 'open to all' existed only in North America, the ex-USSR and a handful of other countries. In Europe, Latin America and much of the rest of the world, the post-elementary model was one of 'differentiated' schooling: different kinds of schools mainly with a vocational orientation alongside a traditional academic secondary school that was not intended (or designed) for mass participation.

Since much of the social demand was for increased access to the traditional secondary school, the opening up of increased opportunities for secondary level education constituted a major challenge for the 'aims and purposes', indeed, the 'very conception of secondary schooling'. The situation in the Netherlands in the early 1950s is a good example of the nature of this challenge: around 10 per cent of primary school leavers entered the traditional academic secondary schools, around 20 per cent continued for two or three years in what was then known as 'advanced' or 'upper' primary education with a pre-vocational orientation, around 25 per cent entered vocational/technical schools, and 45 per cent left school altogether. So long as there were only a limited number of places available in post-elementary education generally, and hence a need to ration the overall demand for places, pressures for reform of post elementary education structures could largely be resisted. However, once the commitment had been adopted to open up opportunities in those countries like the Netherlands that adhered to the 'differentiated' schooling model, the question of which kinds of secondary/post-elementary education to expand could not be avoided, especially since the practice of sorting students into different kinds of schools was arguably at variance with the democratic impulse that was ultimately behind the opening up of opportunities in the first place. In much of the world, therefore, the decades that have passed since the original commitments were adopted to make 'secondary education in its different forms generally available and accessible to all' have been marked by a continuing process of adjustment of secondary education structures to accommodate ever-increasing cohorts of students.

This process has now virtually run its course in the industrial countries and countries in transition, where the secondary gross enrolment ratios are close to, or above 100 per cent, but it is still under way in the majority of countries in the other regions of the world. Sub-Saharan Africa, according to UNESCO's most recent (and still provisional) estimates of net enrolment ratios, is the only region where the absolute number of secondary-school-age youth who are out of school is still growing.

Broadly speaking, and at the risk of oversimplifying the record of what has in fact been a very complex process in most countries from the 1950s to accommodate ever-increasing cohorts of students. This process has now virtually run its course in the industrial countries and countries in transition, where the secondary gross enrolment ratios are close to, or above 100 per cent, but it is still under way in the majority of countries in the other regions of the world. Sub-Saharan Africa, according to UNESCO's most recent (and still provisional) estimates of net enrolment ratios, is the only region where the absolute number of secondary-school-age youth who are out of school is still growing. Broadly speaking, and at the risk of oversimplifying the record of what has in fact been a very complex process in most countries from the 1950s upper secondary schooling while at the same time retaining some provision for separate vocational/ technical schools at the post-compulsory and/or upper stage of secondary education.

In those countries where the 'comprehensive' model already existed, the admission of larger cohorts of students had implications for reform of curricula so as to take into account the wider range of abilities and interests as well as social backgrounds of the students coming into the schools. There were some notable 'holdouts' against the overall trend above towards general secondary education, chiefly the countries of East and Central Europe where secondary-level education at both the lower and upper stages was strongly vocational and technical up until the early 1990s. Moreover, in countries which are still struggling to achieve universal primary education, and which can provide only limited opportunities for secondary level education, a certain amount of provision continues to be made for postprimary vocational education. Even so, there is broad acceptance of the idea of eventually moving towards the provision of a common lower secondary education for all when resources permit.

In a global perspective, the 'comprehensive' model predominates, especially in North America, Asia, the Arab States and sub-Saharan Africa, where the percentages of students enrolled in 'general' secondary schools as opposed to 'vocational/ technical' schools are substantially higher than in Western Europe and the countries in transition, and somewhat higher than in Latin America and the Caribbean.

General Vocational training cational training countries of East and Central Europe. In both the latter region and Western Europe, vocational/ technical programmes are provided today mainly at the upper secondary stage: the average percentage of upper secondary students enrolled in vocational/technical programmes in the fifteen countries of the European Union, for example, is around 60 per cent, although there is variation among individual countries. The corresponding percentage for upper and lower secondary students taken together, is somewhat lower because lower secondary education is predominantly 'general'.

A complete picture of developments in regard to technical and vocational education at the secondary level would require more systematic information on the position of technical and vocational components in the curricula of 'general secondary' (including 'comprehensive') schools than is currently available internationally. The Convention on Technical and Vocational Education, which was drawn up principally with a view to stimulating 'the exchange of information and experiences' and 'strengthening international cooperation in this field', defines technical and vocational education as follows:

> . . . all forms and levels of the educational process involving, in addition to general knowledge, the study of technologies and related sciences and the acquisition of practical skills, know-how, attitudes and understanding relating to occupations in the various sectors of economic and social life (Article 1). It is in this perspective that technical and vocational education have in recent years come to be more clearly recognized as having an essential role to play in 'lifelong learning'.

Equal Opportunity

The principle of 'equal opportunity' has been central to the question of what kinds of education to provide at the secondary level, because of the range of student abilities and interests that need to be catered for. If ideally 'secondary education should be the time when the most varied talents are revealed and flourish', this was hardly possible so long as a majority of young people did not have access to it, which in any case is still the situation in half the countries in the world today.

Both the Convention against Discrimination in Education and later the Convention on the Rights of the Child refer to the general principle of 'equal opportunity' in education. In fact, the Convention against Discrimination in Education was designed in part to promote this principle (actually, 'equality of opportunity and of treatment in the matter of education') and specifically included Article 4 to that effect. The Convention on the Rights of the Child adopts the principle of 'equal opportunity' as the basis of action to be taken by States Parties with a view to achieving the right of the child to education, but implicitly assumes that the various dimensions of this principle are known, presumably because they had already been spelled out earlier in the Convention against Discrimination in Education. Thus, the Convention on the Rights of the Child does not include any wording corresponding to Article 4(b) of the Convention against Discrimination in Education: 'to ensure that the standards of education are equivalent in all public educational institutions of the same level, and that the conditions relating to the quality of education provided are also equivalent'. While the provision of 'equal opportunity' for 'varied talents' to 'flourish' has been as much of a challenge for elementary or primary as for secondary education over the past fifty years, it has generally been a matter of intense concern in secondary education because of the differences in the rewards that societies typically accord to the different types or forms of education at this level. The methods of selection (tests and examinations) utilized in assigning students to different types of secondary education have therefore been the subject of controversy in most countries at one time or another ever since the worldwide expansion of opportunities for secondary level education got under way.

Thus, in the many countries which inherited the 'differentiated' schooling model in secondary/ post-elementary education, the critical factor in generating resistance to further expansion of this model was probably evidence that prevailing selection methods tended to favour the access of children from socially and economically better-off families to the academic secondary schooling that led to higher education, while children from poorer families were channelled towards vocational schooling that was essentially terminal. Educational and economic arguments also were brought to bear: in the former case by demonstrating the uncertainty (if not injustice) inherent in trying to identify children's abilities and interests –and hence life-chances – at too early an age, and in the latter case by demonstrating the uncertainty inherent in trying to predict the economy's future needs for different categories of skills and competencies.

If these reservations have been gradually overcome by the trend in recent decades towards the provision of a general ('basic') education for all at the lower secondary level, it has been because the whole issue of 'equal opportunity' in selection for different types of education has largely been displaced to the upper secondary and tertiary levels. Thus, the policy challenge that existed earlier with respect to opportunities for 12–14 year-old primary school leavers has in more and more countries become one of education/learning opportunities for secondary school leavers who are 16–18 years old or even older.

In those countries that have retained the 'differentiated schooling' model in post-compulsory education at the upper secondary level, chiefly in Europe and to a lesser extent in Latin America and other regions of the world, educational opportunities at this level have essentially been partitioned into schools giving academic programmes that lead directly to higher education, and schools giving vocational/technical programmes that are designed primarily to prepare young people for employment.

In those countries that have adopted the 'comprehensive' model of secondary school-ing, as in North America and much of the rest of the world outside Europe, a similar partitioning can exist within individual schools but is attenuated by the fact that the vocational/ technical pro-grammes of these schools normally do not preclude later access to higher education, for which the basic pre-requisite is usually the successful completion of secondary education as such. If the history of 'differentiated schooling' at the secondary level is any guide to the future, there is likely to be continu-ing pressure from within societies for the removal of boundaries at the tertiary level between educational programmes that foreclose future opportunities for 'lifelong learning' and those that keep such opportunities open.

ICT for Education: Potential and Potency

Social, economic, and technological changes of the past decades are making education and training for all more crucial than ever. Yet, educational systems, to different degrees worldwide, are struggling to afford educational opportunities for all, to provide their graduates with the necessary knowledge and skills for evolving marketplaces and sophisticated living environments, and to prepare citizens for lifelong learning. To meet these challenges, countries have to focus concurrently on expanding access, improving internal efficiency, promoting the quality of teaching and learning, and improving system management. A linear expansion of existing processes and methods may not be sufficient to meet these objectives within a reasonable time.

Some countries and institutions have turned to information and communication technologies (ICTs) and are exploring ways by which ICTs may help them in pursuing their educational goals. This chapter reviews research and experience resulting from these attempts, with a focus on the potential of these technologies to enhance access, efficiency, quality, and management. Frequently, users and experts tend to concentrate on what a specific technology can and cannot do for education. Therefore assessments of the potential and appropriateness of particular technologies must be based on educational needs and objectives, rather than on the technologies themselves.

Education For All

Expanding access to education is a matter of both economic development and social justice. It is true that worldwide illiteracy rates have declined in the past 30 years, but it is also true that the demands on knowledge are much higher now than 30 years ago. In the past, an agrarian society could thrive economically even when more than half of its population was barely literate, but this is no longer possible in modern societies in the Information Age. To remain economically competitive and prosper in this global, knowledge-driven economy, countries cannot afford to have large sectors of their population excluded from education, or at the lower level of the educational process.

Education is positively related to development—that is, a higher proportion of the population of the most developed countries has attained higher educational levels than the population of developing countries. In regions that have stronger economies, such as North America, Western Europe, and parts of Asia, more than half of the college-age youth population is indeed attending college. Tertiary enrollment in the least developed countries is about 3%. Approximately 90 million secondary-school-aged children in Southern Asia were not in school in 2000, and in sub-Saharan Africa, the number of school-aged children who are not in school continues to grow. In many countries, whose budgets already are stretched thin, expanding access to education under traditional models is not an option.

Dramatic conflicts and the burgeoning HIV/AIDS crisis (sometimes occurring simultaneously) in many countries have disrupted social services, including education, and diverted resources that could be used to maintain, let alone, expand educational opportunity. In Togo alone, public expenditure on education already represents 25% of total government expenditures. The country's illiteracy rate for youth aged 15-24 is close to 30% for both genders (45% for girls). A program to eliminate illiteracy that relies on constructing more schools and hiring more teachers will require a level of public investment in Togo that may deplete the country's budget, leaving other essential services unattended.

For more than a century, education has used technology to expand beyond the physical limits of schools and university campuses and reach more and nontraditional groups of students. For instance, in the beginning of the last century, Australia and New Zealand used a system of itinerant teachers to educate children and youth living in sparsely inhabited territories. The teachers maintained contact with their students through postal correspondence.

Radio, television, and computer-related technologies have expanded outreach potential further, and higher education institutions have been at the forefront of this expansion. In 1992, 41% of higher education students in Thailand and 38% in Turkey studied at a distance. The China TV University System and Anadolu University in Turkey each serves more than 500,000 students per year. The United Kingdom Open University has provided education to more than 2 million individuals since it was established about 30 years ago. Distance learning institutions generally use a mix of technologies that may include printed material, videos, video-conferencing, CD-ROMs, e-mail, and the Internet. Many of them start with less expensive technologies, such as printed materials, and move to faster and more powerful resources as the need for expansion increases.

Expanding access also means integrating populations that have been traditionally excluded from education for cultural and social reasons. In cultures with strict rules regarding interaction between genders, girls may be forced to leave school before puberty to avoid contact with male colleagues and teachers. For girls who remain in school, the rules regarding with whom they may or may not talk make it difficult to succeed. If a girl is having academic difficulties, she may rather fail than address the male teacher. Technology can promote alternatives for educating women that are more cost-effective than all-female schools without disrupting cultural traditions.

Television and radio broadcasts or Internet-based technologies enable girls to continue their studies from home or small learning centers. Technology functions as a neutral mediator, without gender or cultural allegiances, thereby facilitating communication. An essay exercise in a coeducational class at the African Nazarene University that required the use of computers illustrates the potential of ICTs to overcome barriers in communication. Faced with the challenge of learning a new technology, the students forgot tribal rivalries and gender differences to exchange information and work side by side.

For persons with disabilities—who represent another significant and forgotten sector of the world population—technologies provide essential supports enabling them to participate in the educational system and the job market. VisualTek is a camera and monitor that enlarge print materials for people with visual disabilities. Voice synthesizers enable individuals with muscular dystrophies to communicate. Special computer software can be used to ameliorate learning disabilities or to enhance the memory of individuals with traumatic brain injury. Keyboard adaptations enable individuals with motor disabilities to write, and the Internet can connect homebound individuals to classrooms and workplaces. Lifelong learning and economic development for populations living outside mainstream cultures are two other venues for using ICTs.

Business organizations are investing heavily in distance learning technologies, particularly Internet-based applications, to train managers and employees while avoiding the costs and disruptions related to travel. The Ford Motor Company spent $100 million on a training network using interactive satellite technology that transmits up to eight live training sessions at a time to any of the 5,000 Ford dealerships across the United States. With the savings in training-related travel costs, the system paid for itself in three years.

The traditional school is, therefore, a physical entity organized into classrooms where learners congregate according to a grade structure and constrained by the limits of space and time. If a school serves students from grades 1 through 12, it must have at least 12 classrooms to accommodate each grade separately. Each classroom must have one teacher. A certain number of teachers require a principal and, often, administrative and teaching support. If the number of students or grades increases, so must the number of needed classrooms, teachers, and support personnel. Generally, beginning in the seventh grade, another dimension is added to the classroom/grade framework: specialization. From then on, the number of teachers is related to both the number of classrooms and the number of specialties offered. Each school must have at least one mathematics teacher, a science teacher, a social studies teacher, and so on. As the educational level

The internal efficiency of an educational system is measured by its ability to deliver quality education in cost-effective ways. The traditional model for providing primary through tertiary education, adopted across the world, relies on three basic principles.

— Learners must congregate in a building where the teaching/learning process takes place.

— There must be a predetermined path, divided into grades, that leads to a diploma, and students must follow this path, regardless of their interests, needs, or abilities.

— There must be a hierarchic structure where the instructor is the provider of knowledge and the students are the recipients become a success story about the power of television to expand access and improve education in cost-effective ways.

Student-Centered Curricula

Traditional educational systems also tend to rely on curricula that were developed at the beginning of the Industrial Revolution and are now disconnected from the realities of the job market. For bright students, these systems offer little in the way of motivation. Eventually, a few extraordinary students will be able to skip a grade, but rushing through the system is not encouraged, and early graduates may find obstacles when they attempt to gain access to the next level. For low-income students, who have less academic support, the schools offer even less: the wealthier schools lure the best teachers, leaving the least prepared for schools in poor and remote areas. When the need to work conflicts with schools' requirements, the student sees no reason to stay in school. As a result, these systems perpetuate social inequalities, lose many excellent students to boredom, increase the costs of education through high dropout rates and grade retention, and pass on to employers or other systems the costs of retraining their graduates.

ICTs have the potential to bring the products of the best teachers to classrooms anywhere in the world. For self-motivated, disciplined students, ICTs can speed the path toward a degree and expand their learning options through self-study. Students can "shop" courses on the Internet and choose their own program of study and schedules. Students in virtual schools can take extra online courses to graduate earlier or fulfill specific interests and curiosity. For those who need to balance studies with work and family obligations—full- or part-time workers, parents of small children, homebound individuals—this flexibility may be most cost-effective for them.

The management of distance learning projects is not without difficulty, and, in many cases, local regulations function as obstacles to innovations. However, the demand for more and specialized education is encouraging new arrangements that rely on ICTs to establish communication networks among partner institutions and facilitate student-centered, rather than program-centered organizations, such as the University of the Highlands and Islands.

Quality of Learning

Research on brain physiology and cognitive psychology is challenging the traditional model of learning as mastery of advances, classroom organizations will rely more on specialization than grades, but the framework is maintained. To be cost-effective within this structure, the learning place must have a critical number of students that justifies school construction and maintenance, particularly personnel costs. In areas of low population density, building and maintaining schools to serve the traditional paradigm is economically prohibitive. The requirement of one specialist per specialty makes secondary schools an even more expensive venture.

Some countries sidestep the problem by leaving the solution to individual families, with catastrophic results. If the families choose to move to urban areas and ensure their children's education, they jeopardize their country's fragile economic balance and further deplete the economy of their native regions. If they decide to remain, they jeopardize their children's future. Areas of high population density but weak economy are not free of problems. In this case, the traditional model encourages administrators to accommodate as many students as possible in one classroom to control personnel costs, which leads to over-crowded and unsafe environments that are unfit for learning.

Learning Time vs. Classroom Time

The capacity of ICTs to reach students in any place and at any time has the potential to promote revolutionary changes in the traditional educational paradigm. First, it eliminates the premise that learning time equals classroom time. To avoid overcrowded classrooms, a school may adopt a dual-shift system without reducing its students' actual study time. Students may attend school for half a day and spend the other half involved in educational activities at home, in a library, at work, or in another unconventional setting. They may be required to watch an educational radio/television programme and complete related activities, or work on a computer-assisted lesson at the school technology lab or in a community learning center. For areas with low population density, multigrade schools become viable alternatives. While more advanced students listen to an educational program on the radio or watch a television broadcast, the teacher can attend to the students who are in less advanced levels or vice versa.

Latin America began experimenting with television to bring education to rural, low-population areas as early as the 1960s. In 1964, the Mexican government tried television as an alternative to provide secondary education (grades 7-9) for children in rural communities. Telesecundaria was created to respond to the needs of rural areas where a general secondary school (grades 7-9) was not feasible, because there were not enough students and it was difficult to attract teachers.

The acquisition of knowledge encompasses mōre than cognition. Perception, for instance, includes at least two basic components:

i) an objective component mediated through the senses, which provide the brain with information about the objects surrounding us, their descriptions and location, and our position in relation to them; and

ii) a subjective component that analyzes the perceived objects through the lens of personal experiences and idiosyncrasies, previous knowledge, and cultural biases.

The process involves both imageries—the mental reconstructions of objects no longer present to our senses, and imagination—the mental construction of unknown objects. In addition to their role in retention and recall, images have the ability to decode unfamiliar symbols into known representations, a helpful function in language acquisition. Textbook images traditionally have been used in foreign language classes with this decoding function. Images are equally important in the acquisition of science and mathematics, which, similar to a foreign language, have their own symbols, terminologies, and grammatical structures.

Although definitions of quality learning may disagree on details, it is generally accepted that, for learning to occur, the learners must be motivated, basic concepts must be understood, and knowledge must be advanced through more complex, higher-order thinking skill tasks. ICTs diversify the systems of representation through the use of various types of stimuli (images, sound, and movement) and address the needs of diverse types of learning (visual, psychomotor, and affective). In addition, ICTs have the potential to enhance educational quality by increasing motivation, facilitating acquisition of basic skills, promoting inquiry and exploration, and preparing individuals for the technology-driven world.

Motivating to Learn

An effective teaching/learning process must stimulate intellectual curiosity and offer a sense of enjoyment that will move the students from the passive role of recipients of information to the active role of builders of knowledge.

Yet, engaging the learner in this process can be the most challenging task for teachers. ICTs are effective instructional aides to engage students in the learning process. Videos, television, and computer multimedia software provide information that can be authentic and challenging in addition to stimulating students' sensorial apparatus through images, color, sound, and movement. Although radio programs do not have the visual appeal of television or computer, Interactive Radio Instruction (IRI) uses songs, drama-like plots, and comic situations to attract and maintain the attention of students of all ages in rural and low-income areas of developing countries.

Transmission of accumulated knowledge to new generations is an essential component of the educational process. This includes basic skills and information that are at the foundation of more complex knowledge. It would be inefficient to use a time-consuming process, such as inquiry and exploration, to transmit basic information. In addition, nonstructured learning environments based solely on inquiry and exploration may be confusing and overwhelming for some children and youth. These students will do better in well-structured classrooms, where the information is broken into less complex units, thus making it easier to understand. Exposition and practice strategies help to structure the classroom, enhance retention and recall, and cut learning time.

Educational television programs, such as Sesame Street, apply repetition and reinforcement to teach children about letters, numbers, or colors. Computers have three attributes that make them powerful aides for drill and practice strategies: large memory, speed, and the capacity to repeat the same task an infinite number of times without reducing performance. In addition, they provide students with the opportunity to learn on their own time and at their own pace. Computer-aided instruction (CAI) has been used successfully in different settings for basic skill instruction. CAI programs are divided into modules that maintain a hierarchy of concepts and skills. The students have to master each module before being allowed to move to the next, more complex level. An evaluation at the end of each module gives the students immediate feedback. If they respond correctly to a determined percentage of questions, they advance.

Otherwise, they repeat the module or enter remedial units until the skills or concepts are mastered. The program can keep a history of the students' performance—lessons learned, topics with which the student had more difficulty, strategies that improved learning, and how many times the student had to repeat the module. With this information, the teacher can develop an individualized plan that addresses each student's specific weaknesses and strengths. CAI was introduced as an aid in mathematics classes, but it is now used for different disciplines, grade levels, and objectives.

Computers also can be used as auxiliary tools in mathematics and science classes to free teachers' and students' time. While computers work on repetitive tasks (such as long calculations and statistical computations), teachers and students can concentrate on analytical activities that require higher-order thinking skills.

Elementary and secondary school students who use calculators have higher test scores and better attitudes toward mathematics than their peers who do not use calculators. Elementary school children who use computers and calculators in the classroom were found to understand mathematical concepts much earlier than expected.

Although basic skills and information are essential components of the teaching/learning process, learning is more than information transfer. Learning requires the ability to analyze 35 and synthesize information, use it in diverse circumstances, and propose new lines of inquiry that foster knowledge. Inquiry and exploration are essential strategies to attain those abilities. ICTs have the potential to restore curiosity to education. ICTs can take students on exciting journeys through time and space. Movies, videos, audio technology, and computer animations bring sound and movement to static textbook lessons and enliven children's reading classes. They also provide social studies and foreign language students with vicarious experiences of distant societies and bygone times. Spreadsheets can store and analyze large amounts of data necessary for complex math and science studies.

Computer simulations transform risky and expensive experiments into safe and cost-effective procedures. The Internet offers virtual reality settings where students can manipulate parameters, contexts, and scenarios. Computer simulations are a good example of the power of technology to improve the learning process. The flight simulator has been used for decades as the initial step in training airplane pilots. A flight simulator offers trainees the opportunity to practice the proper skills to control the plane and deal with emergency situations without risking lives or property loss. Although flight simulators can be complex and expensive machines, no pilot training program would question their utility. Simulators also are becoming essential tools in medical training. Through their use, medical students and residents are introduced to risky and invasive procedures without endangering patients' lives or exposing them to unnecessary pain and discomfort. Simulations are particularly helpful in situations that are too risky, expensive, or time-consuming to allow real-life experiments.

For instance, welding simulators have proved to be a cost-effective method to train future welders. Without simulators, this training requires long hours of practice and burning expensive electrodes. Simulations also enable students to test explosive materials virtually without running the risk of real explosions, and to experiment on animals without the ethical implications of real-life procedures. For elementary and secondary school students—and sometimes even for adults—exploring the Internet can be a fun and enriching experience, or a frustrating adventure in trivia. Teachers and instructors play an important role as guides and facilitators by providing background material and guidelines for the search. They also need to monitor the process, particularly for younger students, who tend to browse the Web, rather than follow structured search plans.

Teachers and instructors also are instrumental in helping students to separate unreliable sources from reliable ones and make sense of the large amount of information that may overwhelm them.

Globalization, creativity, and collaboration are key words in the modern workplace, where employers and employees are expected to share knowledge and work together toward common goals. In traditional classrooms, students work in isolation, doing tasks that emphasize conformism and boost competition. Trained in such environments, students may leave the school ill prepared to share ideas, divide tasks, or accept different points of view. Since ICTs can overcome physical and geographical barriers and facilitate communication, they have the potential to eliminate the artificial boundaries between schools and the outside world, and promote an environment that emphasizes collaboration rather than competition.

Videos and computer animations enable students to 'witness' a volcano eruption to learn about pressure, rock formation, or psychological and sociological responses to crises. A simple radio or tape recorder can allow students in a foreign language class to listen to native speech regardless of their teachers' origin. Better yet, with interactive technologies, such as two-way radios or video-conferencing, students can communicate with native speakers without leaving their classrooms.

Videos, DVDs, computer software, and the Internet bring to schools anywhere in the world information that can be obtained only through the use of powerful scientific instruments that no single school can afford. More than any other technology, the Internet opens new opportunities for collaborative work. From group discussions to full collaborative research projects, the Internet has the potential to connect classrooms to research centers and students to actual scientists, as does the Global Learning and Observations to Benefit the Environment (GLOBE). Research on the Apple Classrooms of Tomorrow (ACOT) indicates that technology—rich classrooms promote teamwork and encourage tolerance for alternative viewpoints, two essential skills for increasingly complex and diverse workplaces.

Teacher training learning is only one component of the educational process, and quality learning cannot be attained without good teaching. Yet, teachers in general, and good teachers in 36 particular, are in short supply even in developed countries. For developing countries, in rural areas and in some specialties such as math and science, the teacher shortage has become critical. Simply hiring a teacher does not ensure quality education. To be effective, teachers must keep abreast of new perspectives on learning theories and their area of specialization, a task that becomes impossible when teachers work in distant, isolated areas. The mentoring process that has been used traditionally to prepare new cadres is an extra burden on experienced teachers, particularly in places where they are already in short supply. Some schools of education are using videotaped sessions to prepare new teachers to enter the classroom without relying solely on mentors.

The process frequently involves videotaping experienced teachers during regular classroom time. Student teachers observe their experienced peers in action, analyzing in detail the strategies used to present the material and interact with the students. The trainees then practice mock lessons with a group of peers or volunteer students while being videotaped. Peers and instructors review the tapes, highlighting weaknesses and strengths and making suggestions for improvement. Only after completing this process is the student teacher sent into actual classrooms. Videos can also be used to analyze teaching styles and idiosyncrasies and help educational systems to change their approaches.

ICTs can be used as tools for training and support of teachers, regardless of their geographical dispersion. Scripted lessons in conjunction with educational programs via radio and television. The use of technology for teacher training has at least three major advantages: it reduces travel costs, avoids disrupting classroom routines, and familiarizes the teachers with the technology.

The Internet has myriad Websites to help teachers develop or improve lesson plans, exchange ideas, obtain information, and find free animations and simulations to enliven their lessons. Most Internet-based collaborative learning projects include teacher support and training, and conference proceedings are published regularly on the Web. Chat rooms or forums may become a laboratory for new ideas. Indeed, contrary to the notion that technology is replacing the teacher, ICTs have expanded the quantity and quality of resources available to making teaching a less lonely endeavor.

Teacher Empowerment

More important still, research indicates that the introduction of ICTs for educational purposes has the potential to bring positive changes to teaching practices. In a survey of more than 2,000 teachers and school principals across the United States, the teachers stated that the technology helped them to become more effective (92% of respondents) and creative (88%). Both teachers and administrators agreed that technology had reinforced instruction, and functioned as a motivator for the students, who were more prone to ask questions and participate in the lessons.

Despite this potential for training and support, ICTs have not been accepted easily among teachers. Some complain that scripted lessons take away their ability to address students' individual differences and improve their own teaching strategies. Others fear that technologies will reduce the role of teachers in defining curriculum and educational strategies, or totally replace them.

Education policy development is an intricate process that requires reliable, timely, user-friendly data. ICTs can be valuable for storing and analyzing data on education indicators; student assessments; educational, physical, and human infrastructure; and cost and finance. The use of computer-related technology is particularly helpful in this field. For instance, administrators and policy makers can construct virtual scenarios around different policy options to determine needs and analyze potential consequences. Each scenario can be analyzed and evaluated systematically, not only in terms of its educational desirability, but also in terms of financial affordability, feasibility, and sustainability over a sufficient period of time to show results. The same elements of computing and telecommunications equipment and service that have made businesses more efficient and cost-effective can be applied to schools and educational systems.

ICTs can help administrators and school principals to streamline operations, monitor performance, and improve use of physical and human resources. More than other technologies, computer-related technologies have the potential to support the management of complex, standards-related instructional processes in relatively simple ways. They also can promote communication among schools, parents, central decision makers, and businesses, thus fostering accountability, public support, and connectivity with the marketplace.

The effectiveness of ICTs—the realization of their potential—depends to a large extent on the context and quality of application. Moreover, since ICTs are only tools for education, it is difficult to isolate the factors that may be contributing to a positive result—such as educational philosophy, quality of teaching, parent support, and students' characteristics. With these caveats in mind, evidence from large studies and meta-analyses suggests that use of ICTs, particularly computer technologies, is correlated to positive academic outcomes, including higher test scores, better attitudes toward schools, and better understanding of abstract concepts.

A longitudinal study of a statewide experiment with computers in the classroom found that those most in need of help—low-income, low-achieving students, and students with disabilities—made the most gains. In addition to better performance in traditional measures of academic achievement, a secondary benefit of ICTs in education is to familiarize new generations with the technologies that have become integral components of the modern world. However, research on the effect of ICTs on academic achievement continues to be open to criticism (as with all other areas of education). Critics deny positive findings as the result of flawed studies, while supporters promote positive results without sufficiently evaluating the quality of the studies. In the final analysis, ICTs are as good as how they are used. The path from potential to effectiveness is neither easy nor automated.

Bibliography

Becker, H. J. "How Exemplary Computer-Using Teachers Differ from Other Teachers: Implications for Realizing the Potential of Computers in Schools." *Journal of Research on Computing in Education,* 25, 291-320., 1994.

____________ ., "Teaching With and About Computers in Secondary Schools." *Communications of the ACM,* 36, 69-73. 1993.

Cuban, *Oversold and Underused: Computers in the Classroom,* London:Harvard University Press, 2001.

Kaufman, R., & Watkins, R., "Assuring the Future of Distance Learning", *The Quarterly Review of Distance Education,* 1 (1): 59-67, 2000.

Savita Rastogi, *Teacher's Development in Higher Education.* New Delhi, Classical, 2001.

Simonson, M., "Teaching and Learning at a Distance: Foundations in Distance Education", Columbus, OH: Prentice-Hall.; 2000.

Stufflebeam, D., "Educational evaluation and decision making", Illinois: Peacock, 1971.

Stenhouse, L., *An Introduction to Curriculum Research and Development.* London: Heinemann, 1975.

Torres, R. M., "Teacher education: From rhetoric to action", *In Partnerships in teacher development for a new Asia,* Bangkok: UNESCO/PROAP, 1996.

Twining, 'Making Barriers Explicit: Some problems with the computer innovation literature', in Willis, Robins & Willis (eds), *Technology and Teacher Education Annual 1995*, pp.879-885, Association for the Advancement of Computing in Education, 1995.

Twining, "ICT and the nature of learning: implications for the design of a distance education course", in Paechter, Edwards, Harrison & Twining (Eds), *Learning, Space and Identify*, London: Paul Chapmen Publishing Ltd., 2001.

UNESCO, *International Conference on Education*, 1996.

______________, ILO, *Recommendation Concerning the Status of Teachers*, 1984.

Index